A PH

D0588869

FLOWERS
OF SOUTH AFRICA

BRAAM VAN WYK

Struik Publishers (Pty) Ltd
(a member of The Struik New Holland Publishing Group (Pty) Ltd)
Cornelis Struik House
80 McKenzie Street
Cape Town 8001
Reg. No.: 54/00965/07

First published 2000

10 9 8 7 6 5 4 3 2 1

Publishing manager: Pippa Parker
Managing editor: Simon Pooley
Editor: Gary Lyon
Designer: Dominic Robson
Cartographer: Genene Hart

Reproduction by Hirt and Carter Cape (Pty) Ltd
Printed and bound by Tien Wah Press (Pte) Ltd

ISBN 1 86872 390 9

Cover, front: Bush lily (p.60) (Braam van Wyk); back: Blue waterlily
(p.129) (Tony Pooley). Title page: *Protea cynaroides*, the king sugar-
bush, floral emblem of South Africa (Nigel Dennis). The 'flower' is in
fact a flowerhead composed of numerous white flowers, surrounded
by showy, usually pink to red bracts. About 85 species of *Protea*
(sugarbushes) occur in South Africa; all are woody plants, and most
of the more conspicuous ones are shrubs or small trees (not the focus
of this book).

Acknowledgements
My thanks to all those who made it possible for this book to be produced, especially those who contributed photographs. Many thanks to
Anne Stadler who prepared the line drawings used in the glossary. My
appreciation to Martie Dednam, Elsa van Wyk, Elizabeth Retief and
Elsa Pooley, who assisted in various ways with the preparation of the
manuscript. The National Botanical Institute is thanked for the use of
plant distribution data from the National Herbarium, Pretoria (PRE)
Computerized Information System (PRECIS); I am indebted to Han-
nelie Snyman for her assistance. Many thanks to Pippa Parker, Gary
Lyon, Dominic Robson, Simon Pooley, Colette Stott and Carmen
Watts at Struik Publishers for their patience and support.

CONTENTS

For a country of its size South Africa's floristic and vegetational diversity is without equal in the world; over 22 000 plant species are native to the region. Many South African plants are strikingly beautiful and several popular garden ornamentals are derived from species native to the region. The principal objective of this book is to give the reader a glimpse of the region's floral riches. Common and conspicuous plant species that are likely to be seen, especially along the roadside, have been featured in this book. The species included represent all the major vegetation types and include several weedy alien species that are naturalised in the region. Though this book covers many flowering plant species, inhabiting a range of vegetation types, it describes only a fraction of the species found in South Africa. Those who want more information on our flora are referred to related books on the topic, some of which are listed under 'Further reading' (see page 141).

South Africa has two distinct floristic kingdoms and is one of only a few countries in the world where one can drive overland from one kingdom to another; it certainly is the one where the change in species composition is most noticeable and the transition between two kingdoms most striking. South Africa is also the only country in the world to harbour an entire floristic kingdom, namely, the Cape Floristic Kingdom. The smallest kingdom by far, the Cape Floristic Kingdom has more than 8 000 plant species, at least 70% of which are strictly confined to the region. Groups that contribute extensively to the floristic diversity of the Cape are the ericas (730 species) and especially the families Proteaceae (proteas), Restionaceae (reeds), Iridaceae (irises), Asteraceae (daisies), Rutaceae (buchus), Fabaceae (legumes) and Mesembryanthemaceae (vygies). No less than eight plant families are more or less strictly confined to the Cape.

Outside the Cape, the flora of South Africa has a very different composition and is classified as part of the Palaeotropical Kingdom, a large floristic region that includes most of Africa, Madagascar, India, Malaysia and Indonesia. Prominent groups within this region are from families such as Poaceae (grasses), Mimosaceae (acacia family), Combretaceae (bush willow family), Convolvulaceae (morning glory family), Acanthaceae (acanthus family), Malvaceae (hibiscus family) and many others with a more tropical affinity.

BIOMES

Vegetation can be described as the general effect produced by the growth forms of some or all the plant species in combination. Worldwide the principal vegetation types are forest, savanna, thicket, grassland, semidesert, desert and fynbos (sclerophyllous shrubland). Development of these broad groupings, which represent different habitats, is determined by prevailing climatic conditions over large areas. It is mainly the structural features of a vegetation type that determine its associated macrofauna (e.g. birds, mammals).

Areas relatively uniformly covered by any one of these broad vegetation types usually represent major biotic zones called biomes. Although biomes are not determined floristically, they do contain characteristic plant species adapted to the specific prevailing habitat conditions. South Africa has seven biomes (see map), which are briefly described below. By also considering floristic differences, the biomes are further divided into about 70 different vegetation types.

BIOMES OF SOUTH AFRICA, LESOTHO AND SWAZILAND

- ■ Forest
- ■ Thicket
- ░ Savanna
- □ Grassland
- ░ Nama-Karoo
- ░ Succulent Karoo
- ░ Fynbos

Forest Biome

Dominated by woody vegetation, a forest is multilayered with a continuous canopy cover. South Africa is very poorly endowed with forest; it is by far the smallest biome, covering less than 0.25% of the region. Forests usually occur as small, isolated patches (rarely larger than 1 km²) in relatively frost-free areas with a mean annual rainfall of usually more than 725 mm. South Africa's forest can be divided into three main types: Afromontane, Coastal and Sand forest. These forests are rather poor in wild flowers, with many of the more colourful species occurring as shrublets or creepers along forest margins. Among the more conspicuous flowers on the shady forest floor are species of *Clivia*, *Dietes*, *Plectranthus* and *Streptocarpus*. A few epiphytic orchids, usually with white flowers, occur in the tree canopies.

Grassland Biome

Grassland is found chiefly on the eastern half of the high central plateau of South Africa and the inland regions of KwaZulu-Natal and the Eastern Cape. These are summer-rainfall regions. Frost, fire and grazing maintain the grass dominance and prevent the establishment of trees. Although dominated by a single layer of perennial grasses, the majority of plant species in this biome are non-grassy herbs, most of which are perennial plants that sprout annually from large underground storage structures. Among the more showy plants are the so-called pre-rain flowers. These appear in spring before the first rains, especially following veld fires. Unfortunately, commercial afforestation and ploughing have already destroyed large parts of the biome.

Savanna Biome

Savanna covers about one-third of South Africa and is the largest biome in the region. It is confined to areas with summer rainfall and an often subtropical climate. The vegetation is characterised by a grassy ground layer with varying densities of emergent trees. Where the trees are tall and dense, the vegetation is often referred to as woodland. A more open parkland with smaller trees and shrubs is locally known as bushveld. Fire is an important natural factor, the absence of which may result in bush encroachment. Wild flowers of this region are usually perennials, with annuals becoming more prominent in arid types of savanna, such as Mopane Bushveld.

Thicket Biome

Thicket is characterised by dense, deciduous or evergreen shrubs, with a few trees rising above, and lacks a conspicuous grass cover. Constituent plants are often spiny and/or thorny. It is sometimes classified under the Savanna Biome. Some of its variations are referred to as Valley Bushveld. This biome is mainly confined to hot, arid river valleys in subtropical regions along the east coast. Wild flowers are conspicuous, many being perennial climbers or scramblers, whereas succulents and bulbous plants are common in the undergrowth.

Nama-Karoo Biome

This is the second largest biome in the region. It occupies the semi-desert summer-rainfall region on the central plateau of the western half of South Africa, known as the Karoo. The vegetation is dominated by perennial, woody shrublets (locally known as *bossies*), interspersed with scattered grasses and other forbs. This is often referred to as karroid vegetation. Many of the shrublets are quite attractive when in full flower, but mass flowering events are erratic and in response to good rains, which may be separated by years of drought.

Succulent Karoo Biome

A semidesert biome confined to areas with a low winter rainfall and extreme summer drought. The vegetation is dominated by dwarf perennial shrublets, many of which are leaf succulents. It is also referred to as karroid vegetation or, on the sandy coastal plains along the west coast, as Strandveld. Floristically the second richest biome after Fynbos, it is the centre of diversity for the vygies (Mesembryanthemaceae) and is rich in geophytes and annuals. Following good rains, annuals often create brightly coloured mass flowering displays on degraded or fallow lands, and are a major tourist attraction.

Fynbos Biome

Fynbos, Afrikaans for 'fine-leaved bush', refers to a vegetation type dominated by evergreen, woody shrubs and shrublets with small, tough and often linear needle-shaped leaves. Also known as sclerophyllous shrubland, this vegetation type is characteristic of regions with a mediterranean-type climate (winter rain and summer drought). Based on floristic composition, two main vegetation groupings occur in this biome, namely Renosterveld on nutrient-rich clayey soils and Fynbos (not to be confused with the Fynbos Biome) on nutrient-poor sandy soils. The Cape Floristic Kingdom is fairly congruent with the Fynbos Biome, which has over one-third of all the plant species in South Africa; it is the only one of the world's six floristic kingdoms comprising only a single broad vegetation type. This region is world-famous for its floristic diversity and abundance of showy wild flowers, notably Proteaceae, Ericaceae, Asteraceae and Iridaceae.

HOW TO USE THIS BOOK

This book covers South Africa, Lesotho and Swaziland ('the region'). Species have been grouped into six main colour sections, based on the general colour impression of the flower (or what the layman may take as the flower). Within each colour section, the species appear alphabetically according to family, the latter also arranged in alphabetical sequence. Each species entry starts with the accepted scientific name, family name and an English and Afrikaans common name. In a few cases the scientific name is followed by recent synonyms in brackets. An asterisk* indicates an alien species. Peak flowering time is given in the form of seasonal indicators: spring = August–November; summer = November–March; autumn = March–May; winter = May–August. Descriptive text for each species is restricted to brief comments on habit, habitat and some of the plant's more obvious morphological features. This is followed by notes on the species, including aspects such as behaviour, interaction with other organisms, importance to man, classification and reference to related species. Each species description has a colour photograph of the flowers (in a few cases also the fruit), and a range-style distribution map. Green shaded areas on the map serve as a rough guide to the core distribution area of a particular species. Technical terms are explained in the glossary (page 138), or in line drawings below and on page 140.

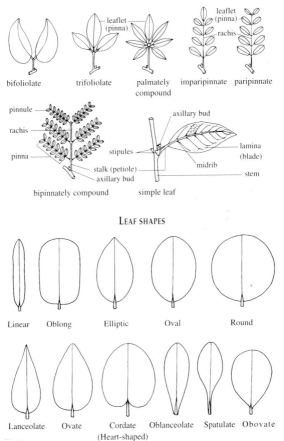

SIMPLE AND COMPOUND LEAVES

bifoliolate

trifoliolate — leaflet (pinna)

palmately compound — leaflet (pinna)

imparipinnate — leaflet (pinna), rachis

paripinnate

bipinnately compound — pinnule, rachis, pinna, stalk (petiole), axillary bud

simple leaf — axillary bud, stipules, midrib, lamina (blade), stem

LEAF SHAPES

Linear   Oblong   Elliptic   Oval   Round

Lanceolate   Ovate   Cordate (Heart-shaped)   Oblanceolate   Spatulate   Obovate

Haemanthus albiflos

Amaryllidaceae   Autumn–Winter   White paintbrush / Witpoeierkwas

Evergreen, clump-forming perennial, up to 400 mm high, with a bulb; occurring in forest and thicket, usually in coastal areas. Leaves 2–4, strap-shaped, smooth or hairy. Flowers in a dense umbel (or 'brush'), ± 30 mm long, surrounded by green bracts; perianth white; anthers yellow. Fruit a berry, oval, red when ripe. Bulbs located just below or even partly above soil surface. Some forms have leaves with white spots. Bulb used for medicinal and magical purposes. Both leaves and bulbs have been shown to be effective against certain viruses. *H. pauculifolius*, a rare species from northwestern KwaZulu-Natal and Mpumalanga, has mostly a single leaf, longer umbels (up to 55 mm), and flowers with the perianth lobes more spreading.

Braam van Wyk

Aponogeton distachyos

Aponogetonaceae   Winter–Spring   Cape pondweed / Waterblommetjie

Perennial aquatic herb, with a tuber; occurring in dams, rivers and ditches. Leaves floating, lanceolate to oblong, 60–200 x 20–70 mm, with a long stalk. Flowers in forked spikes, arranged in 2 rows on the upper surface, white, sweetly scented. Each flower subtended by a large, bract-like petal. Confined to the winter-rainfall area; plants survive as tubers when water dries up. Flowering spikes edible during various stages of development; when in bud, with open flowers, or with young fruit, the older spikes being firmer and less watery. The plant is cultivated commercially; flowers marketed fresh or canned. They are cooked with mutton to produce a delicious stew known as *waterblommetjie bredie*. Also used in salads and soups. The tubers, which are rich in starch, are also edible.

John Manning

Zantedeschia aethiopica

Araceae   Spring–Summer

White arum lily

Witvarkoor

Deciduous or evergreen perennial, up to 1.5 m high, with a rhizomatous tuber; occurring in fynbos, grassland, bushveld and along forest margins, usually in wet places. Leaves broadly ovate-cordate, usually unspotted. Flowers borne on a yellow spadix, 50–75 mm long, which is subtended by a large spathe, male and female, without petals or sepals; spathe funnel-shaped, white inside, without a purple blotch at base (see arrow-leaved arum). Female flowers at base of spadix interspersed by sterile stamens. A popular garden plant; extensively grown as a cut flower, especially in New Zealand, with many cultivars (also known as calla lilies). Leaves cooked as a pot herb in times of famine. Tubers formerly boiled and fed to pigs. Leaves and tubers used in traditional medicine.

John Manning

Zantedeschia albomaculata

Araceae   Summer

Arrow-leaved arum

Witvlekvarkoor

Deciduous perennial, up to 700 mm high, with a discoid tuber; occurring in grassland, bushveld and along forest margins, usually in marshy places. Leaves ± arrow-shaped, with or without white spots. Flowers borne on a yellow spadix, which is subtended by a large spathe, male and female, without petals or sepals; spathe cylindrical, variable in colour, white, cream, or pale yellow inside, usually with a dark purple blotch at base. Female flowers at base of spadix not interspersed by sterile stamens. Used in traditional medicine. *Zantedeschia*, a genus of eight species, is largely confined to southern Africa. Plants contain abundant, needle-like crystals of calcium oxalate; chewing of raw material causes severe irritation of the mouth and throat.

Olaf Wirminghaus

Arctotis venusta

Asteraceae   Spring–Summer

Free State daisy

Vrystaatse gousblom

Greyish annual herb up to 600 mm high; occurring in grassland and karroid vegetation, often in disturbed places such as fallow fields and along roadsides. Leaves crowded near base of plant, elliptic-obovate, with margin deeply toothed to pinnately dissected, greyish green, with white hairs. Flower heads (see page 140) on long, erect stalks, radiate, 70 mm in diameter; ray florets with upper surface white or pale cream, coppery purple to mauve below; disc florets blue-black or purple. A frost-hardy species often cultivated in gardens; sow seed in March for a floral display in spring.

Braam van Wyk

Generic name derived from the Greek *arktos* = a bear, and *otis* = ear, perhaps alluding to the pappus scales on the fruit, the involucral bracts or the shaggy fruit. The specific name means 'beautiful'.

Callilepis laureola

Asteraceae   Spring

Ox-eye daisy

Wildemagriet

Perennial herb, up to 600 mm high, sprouting annually from a woody tuber; occurring in grassland. Leaves linear-lanceolate to lanceolate, ± 65 × 20 mm, 3-veined; margin smooth or toothed. Flower heads (see page 140) solitary at the ends of erect stalks, radiate, ± 60 mm in diameter; ray florets white or creamy white; disc florets purplish black. Flowering is stimulated by veld fires. Well known under the Zulu name *Impila*, the tuber is extensively used in traditional medicine as a powerful remedy to treat numerous ailments. Use of the plant for these purposes should, however, be discouraged.

Wally Menne

The tuber is highly toxic, inducing both liver and renal necrosis, with often fatal results. *C. leptophylla,* which mainly occurs in Highveld grassland, has needle-like leaves.

Dimorphotheca pluvialis

Asteraceae　　　　Winter–Spring　　　　Cape rain daisy / Witbotterblom

Annual herb, up to 300 mm high, often branching from the base; occurring in strandveld, fynbos and karroid vegetation, often on sandy soils. Leaves alternate, strap-shaped, ± 70 mm long; margin coarsely and bluntly toothed. Flower heads (see page 140) occur singly at the ends of erect stalks, up to 70 mm in diameter, radiate; ray florets glistening white above, with a narrow purple band at the base, mauve below; disc florets purplish black or yellow. Form brilliant patches in disturbed sandy areas in spring. Popular annual for mass planting in gardens, often combined with yellow and orange forms of *D. sinuata*. The violet ring around the centre varies in width, being much more noticeable in some cultivated forms. Plants may cause prussic-acid poisoning in sheep.

John Manning

Eriocephalus africanus

Asteraceae　　　　Winter–Spring　　　　Wild rosemary / Kapokbossie

A greyish, much-branched perennial shrublet, up to 1 m high; occurring in karroid vegetation and strandveld. Leaves alternate or in tufts, needle-like or 3–5-lobed, ± 15 mm long, greyish. Flower heads (see page 140) in dense clusters towards the ends of stems, radiate; ray florets petal-like, 2–5, white; disc florets reddish purple. Fruiting heads have a very conspicuous fluffy covering, resembling bits of cotton-wool. Leaves pleasantly aromatic; grazed by livestock, giving their milk a characteristic flavour. Fluffy heads once used to fill pillows. Formerly one of the favourite nest-building materials of the Cape penduline tit (a small bird), now also supplemented by wool from sheep. These remarkable nests have a false entrance that remains open; the true entrance can be closed.

Braam van Wyk

11

Felicia muricata (= *Aster muricatus*)

Asteraceae

Spring–Autumn

White felicia

Karooblommetjie

A bushy perennial herb with a woody base, up to 400 mm high; occurring in grassland and karroid vegetation, proliferating in overgrazed places. Leaves in axillary tufts, narrowly strap-shaped, ± 15 × 1 mm. Flower heads (see page 140) on leafless stalks at the tips of branches, radiate, ± 15 mm in diameter; ray florets ± backward-pointing, white or mauve; disc florets yellow. Ray florets tend to be mauve in karroid areas, white in grassland. They point backwards at night and move upwards during daylight. Palatable and well grazed by livestock. Used in traditional medicine; fresh material is crushed and the scent inhaled to relieve headache. Also used to treat cows that are ill after calving. About 70 species of *Felicia* occur in the region, the majority with blue or mauve ray florets.

Braam van Wyk

Metalasia muricata

Asteraceae

All year

White bristle bush

Witsteekbos

A much-branched, rounded shrub or small tree, with erect branches; oc-curring in fynbos, strandveld and grassland, often along streams or among rocks. Branchlets white-felted. Leaves in tufts or scattered, stalkless, needle-like, somewhat twisted, up to 18 × 2 mm, sharp-tipped, often with white, woolly hairs; margin rolled downward. Flowers in branched, terminal heads (see page 140), white, often tinged pink or purple, sweetly scented. Plays a useful role in the stabilisation of coastal dunes. Leaves and twigs are brewed as a tea. Used in Lesotho, sometimes with other plants, as a fumigant during illness or after a death. Despite the hard, spiny leaves it is eaten by sheep. Utilised as a fuel in areas where wood is scarce. More than 50 species of *Metalasia* are native to the region.

John Manning

Osmitopsis asteriscoides

Asteraceae   All year

Mountain daisy

Belskruie

A slender, sparsely branched perennial shrublet, up to 2 m high, lower parts of stems leafless; occurring in fynbos, usually as dense stands in swampy places. Leaves stalkless, lanceolate, up to 80 x 18 mm, velvety and somewhat sticky because of glandular hairs. Flower heads (see page 140) radiate, up to 35 mm in diameter, clustered on short side branches near the tips of main stems; ray florets white; disc florets yellow. Crushed leaves with strong camphor smell, due to a volatile oil rich in camphor and eucalyptol. Traditional Cape-Dutch remedy for a variety of ailments, including chest complaints, stomach problems, inflammation, body pains, paralysis, cuts, swellings, fever and influenza; usually administered as a brandy tincture (*belsbrandewyn*) or small bags of dried herb for external use.

Ben-Erik van Wyk

Syncarpha vestita (= *Helichrysum vestitum*)

Asteraceae   Summer

Cape everlasting

Kaapse sewejaartjie

A robust, woolly perennial shrublet, up to 1 m high; occurring in fynbos, usually in sandy soils derived from sandstone. Leaves closely arranged, narrow, greyish green, soft, thickly covered with white felt. Flower heads (see page 140) borne singly on erect stalks, ± 50 mm in diameter, silvery white, with a purple or maroon centre. Flower heads are very attractive, even when still in bud. Extensively collected for use in dried-flower arrangements; scarce in some areas due to over-picking. Flower heads of *Helichrysum* are very similar to those of *Syncarpha* and *Edmondia* (both confined mainly to the Western Cape). A useful field character is that the leaf margins in the latter two genera are often rolled upwards, at least towards the tip, but this is not very clear in *S. vestita*.

Braam van Wyk

13

Rhigozum trichotomum

Bignoniaceae   Spring–Summer

Three thorn

Driedoring

A rigid, woody shrublet, up to 2 m high, spreading by means of underground stems; occurring in karroid vegetation, usually in sandy soils. Stems tend to branch in threes, hence the specific name *trichotomum* (Greek) = divided into three. Leaves clustered on short shoots, narrowly egg-shaped, up to 12 × 3 mm, blue-green. Flowers solitary on short shoots, ± stalkless; corolla with a broad tube and 5 spreading lobes, white to pale cream or reddish. Capsule spindle-shaped, up to 100 × 3 mm; seed with transparent wings. Unpalatable to livestock, although flowers and capsules are grazed. Plants proliferate in overgrazed veld, often forming impenetrable thickets; covers thousands of hectares in the northern parts of the Great Karoo and adjacent Kalahari.

Piet van Wyk–Agfa

Heliotropium steudneri

Boraginaceae   Spring–Autumn

Common heliotrope

Hamelstertjie

An erect perennial shrublet, up to 800 mm high; occurring in bushveld and grassland, often in disturbed places. Leaves with short stalks, alternate, simple, lanceolate; margin wavy. Flowers in simple or forked terminal spikes, the latter ± coiled downwards at the tips, with flowers pointing upwards; corolla of 5 fused petals, ± 5 mm in diameter, lobes oblong, with ± rounded or broadly tapering tips, white with a yellow throat. About 15 species of *Heliotropium* are native to the region. They usually have white flowers in markedly curled, 1-sided spikes. *H. ciliatum*, a common species along roadsides, has corolla lobes with hair-like tips. Generic name from the Greek *helios* (the sun) and *trope* (to turn), referring to the old belief that the spikes turned with the sun.

Piet van Wyk–Agfa

Berzelia lanuginosa

Bruniaceae Winter–Spring

Marsh berzelia

Vleiknopbos

Braam van Wyk

Evergreen, erect, much-branched perennial shrub, up to 2 m high; occurring in fynbos, usually in dense stands along watercourses or in marshy places. Branches tend to droop. Leaves ± 0.5 mm wide, needle-like, spreading. Flowers very small, massed together in many rounded heads on branched terminal stems; heads ± 8 mm in diameter, with stalks often swollen and bright red; stamens conspicuously elongated, white to pale cream, giving a fluffy appearance to the heads. Presence of the plants is a good indicator for permanent water. Also known in Afrikaans as *kolkol*, because the localised stands of plants stand out, especially when in flower, as distinct patches (Afrikaans: *kolle*) against the uniform green of the surrounding fynbos. The genus comprises 12 species.

Brunia nodiflora

Bruniaceae Autumn–Winter

Common brunia

Gewone stompie

Colin Paterson-Jones

Evergreen perennial shrublet, up to 1 m high, with a woody rootstock; occurring in fynbos, usually on mountain slopes. Leaves scale-like, up to 3 mm long, closely packed along stems. Flowers very small, clustered into dense, rounded heads, ± 10 mm in diameter; heads surrounded at the base by tightly packed, hairy bracts; stamens elongated and giving a fluffy appearance to the heads, white or pale cream; styles 2 per flower. Fruiting heads greyish, may remain on plants for a year or more. Resprouts after veld fires. Very similar in appearance to *Berzelia*, which has flowers with a single style. With the exception of one very rare species in Pondoland, the Bruniaceae (12 genera and about 80 species) are all confined to the Cape Floristic Region.

Scabiosa columbaria

Dipsacaceae   Spring–Summer

Wild scabiosa

Jonkmansknoop

A Slender perennial herb, up to 1 m high, with a woody rootstock; occurring in grassland and bushveld. Leaves mainly in a basal rosette, the latter spoon-shaped, varying from smooth to toothed margins to deeply lobed; stem leaves smaller, often deeply lobed once or twice. Flowers in long-stalked, flat-topped terminal heads, 25–35 mm in diameter; corolla downy, white, lilac to pink, peripheral ones larger, ± 2-lipped; sepals bristly, persisting on the fruit. Widespread from the Cape up to Ethiopia; also in Europe. The compact inflorescences achieve a much more conspicuous floral display than would scattered solitary flowers; visited by a great variety of pollinators, including bees, beetles, wasps and butterflies. Used in traditional medicine for a variety of ailments.

Braam van Wyk

Dietes grandiflora

Iridaceae   Spring–Summer

Large wild iris

Grootwilde-iris

Evergreen, clump-forming perennial, up to 1.5 m high, with a sturdy, creeping rhizome; occurring in grassland and along forest margins, often in wet places. Leaves erect, sword-shaped, ± 1 000 × 15 mm, dark green. Flowers large (up to 100 mm in diameter), in clusters of 3 or 4 at the ends of irregularly branched, erect stalks; tepals 6, white, outer 3 larger, with a yellow, bearded blotch edged by brownish speckling at the base; style with 3 slightly spreading, leaf-like lobes, each 2-fid, violet. A popular garden plant. Although the flowers are fleeting, each one lasting only one day, new flowers open each day over an extended period of time. *D. iridioides* has flowers up to 60 mm in diameter; occurs in shady places in forest, young plants often developing on old flowering stems.

Braam van Wyk

Gladiolus longicollis

Iridaceae — Spring–Summer

Honey flowers
Graspypie

A slender, erect perennial, up to 800 mm high, with a corm; occurring mainly in grassland. Leaves 3, only the lowermost with a well-developed blade, ± 750 × 5 mm, with 4 narrow, longitudinal grooves. Flowers 1–4 on long, slender, erect stem, opening one at a time; perianth with tube 50–110 mm long, lobes triangular, creamy white inside, often mottled with brown, brownish-speckled on the outside. Flowers open in the late afternoon, or during the day in cool, misty weather. In the evening they release a sweet, penetrating scent, reminiscent of carnations and cloves; pollinated by hawkmoths. Hawkmoth-pollinated flowers are generally pale in colour, with long, nectar-filled floral tubes and a heavy scent in the evening and night, features clearly displayed by this species.

Wally Menne

Becium obovatum

Lamiaceae — Spring–Summer

Cat's whiskers
Katsnor

A low-growing perennial shrublet, up to 300 mm high, with erect, annual, herbaceous stems from a woody rootstock; occurring in grassland and bushveld. Leaves ± stalkless, 15–40 × 5–20 mm, opposite, smooth to hairy. Flowers crowded at the ends of erect stalks; corolla 2-lipped, 10–18 mm long, white to pale mauve, upper lip usually with longitudinal violet lines (nectar guides), rarely pure white; stamens protruding for up to 20 mm, curved upwards. Typical pre-rain flower of the Grassland Biome. Adapted to grassland that is periodically burned; flowers profusely after fire. Crushed leaves have a delicate perfume. An infusion of the pounded root is used to treat stomach troubles; also reputed to be a hair-restorer. Larval food plants for several butterflies of the genus *Lepidochrysops*.

Braam van Wyk & Sasa Malan

Salvia disermas (= *S. rugosa*) Limestone sage

Lamiaceae   Summer   Kalksalie

Perennial herb, up to 500 mm high, with a woody rootstock; occurring in grassland and karroid vegetation, often on limestone. Leaves mainly crowded at base of plant, broadly ovate to oblong-lanceolate, rough and hairy above; venation distinctly raised below; margin irregularly scalloped or toothed. Flowers in whorls of ± 6 towards the ends of erect stalks; corolla 2-lipped, 15–30 mm long, white, pale blue or pale mauve. Strongly aromatic when crushed; widely used in traditional medicine. Leaves and flowers used as a revitalising tea or to bring down fever. Leaves, often mixed with root of *Rubia horrida*, are also used to treat skin disorders. Tend to proliferate in overgrazed veld. Closely related to *S. radula*, the leaves of which are white and woolly below.

Braam van Wyk

Lanaria lanata (= *L. plumosa*) Cape edelweiss

Lanariaceae   Summer   Kapokblom

Erect perennial, up to 800 mm high, with a ± vertical rhizome; occurring in fynbos, especially on rocky mountain slopes in sandy soils derived from sandstone. Leaves in a tussock, tough, narrow, dull green, ± hairless, with ± 9 prominent parallel veins. Flowers small, opening in succession, clustered in much-branched panicles at the end of a sturdy, erect stalk, the whole being densely covered by white, woolly hairs; perianth with 6 lobes, densely hairy outside, mauve and hairless inside. Blooms profusely after fire. Although the individual flowers are mauve, the inflorescence appears white from a distance. The only member of the family; endemic to the Cape Floristic Region. Previously classified under Haemodoraceae. Scientific name from the Latin *lana* = wool.

John Manning

Albuca setosa (= *A. pachychlamys*)

Liliaceae   Spring

Small white albuca

Kleinwitslymstok

Erect, bulbous herb, up to 300 mm high; bulb scales ending in persistent fibres; occurring in grassland and bushveld. Leaves produced after flowering, few, ± 300 mm long, ± 20 mm wide at base. Flowers in racemes, all facing upwards; perianth with 6 lobes, outer 3 spreading, inner 3 converging and hooded at the tips, white, with broad green to greenish brown central stripe on back; stamens concealed by the inner perianth lobes. One of the typical pre-rain flowers of the Grassland Biome. Flowering is stimulated by veld fires; fruit matures exceedingly fast. Leaves and flower stalk rich in slime, hence the Afrikaans common name (*slym* = slime). About 60 species of *Albuca* occur in the region. Flowers mostly white or yellow, very similar-looking; species recognition often difficult.

Braam van Wyk & Sasa Malan

*Lilium formosanum

Liliaceae   Summer

Formosa lily

Formosa-lelie

An erect, single-stemmed perennial, up to 1.5 m high, with a bulb; occurring as a weed in grassland, often along roadsides and in marshy places, especially along the northeastern Drakensberg Escarpment. Leaves arranged all along stem, strap-shaped, ± 180 × 10 mm. Flowers in terminal racemes of 3–10, large (130–200 mm long), slightly drooping; perianth funnel-shaped, white, each segment with a reddish keel. A native of Taiwan (formerly Formosa). Flowers sweetly scented. *Lilium* (± 100 species) represents the true lilies, all of which are from the northern hemisphere; extensively cultivated with many hybrids. *L. candidum* (Madonna lily; Israel, Lebanon and Balkans) cultivated since at least 1500 BC for its white flowers, which are used in scent-making; may be the Rose of Sharon of the Bible.

Braam van Wyk

Urginea altissima (= *U. epigea*)

Liliaceae   Spring

Tall white squill

Reuseslangkop

A slender, erect, deciduous perennial, up to 2.5 m high with a large, thick-scaled bulb, the latter borne above or just below the ground; occurring in bushveld and thicket, usually in dense colonies. Leaves erect, 150–300 × 20–30 mm, leathery, grey-green. Flowers in a raceme at the end of a sturdy, exceptionally long, erect stalk; perianth segments white, with a green or brownish streak down the middle. Leaves produced after flowering. Flowers open early morning, and close by midday. Bulbs used in traditional medicine to treat colds, backache and also for magical purposes. Whole plant highly toxic; active principles include cardiac glycosides, the cause of acute and often fatal poisoning in livestock. Cut bulb rubbed on inner surface of leather skins laid out to dry for tanning; deters dogs.

Braam van Wyk

Mesembryanthemum guerichianum

Mesembryanthemaceae   Spring–Summer

Ice plant

Brakslaai

Annual or short-lived perennial succulent with robust, creeping stems; occurring in fynbos, strandveld and karroid vegetation; often forming dense stands in seasonal streams, flood plains, brackish areas and disturbed places. Most parts covered in glistening, collapsible round cells, specialised for water storage. Leaves large and conspicuous (lettuce-like), folded upwards along the midrib, green, usually tinged red. Flowers in clusters at ends of stems; petals numerous, white, pale yellow or pink. Flowers open in bright sunlight and close at night; pollinated by honeybees. Formerly a solution prepared from dried or fresh leaves was used to remove hair from skins during tanning. May cause oxalate poisoning in sheep and goats, although not readily grazed.

John Manning

Jasminum multipartitum

Oleaceae — Spring–Summer

Common wild jasmine

Gewone wildejasmyn

Perennial, ± climbing shrub, up to 3 m high; occurring in thicket and bushveld, often in rocky places. Leaves opposite, simple, ± hairless; stalk up to 5 mm long, appearing articulated (with knee-like thickening) ± in the middle. Flowers solitary or in clusters at the ends of main and side twigs; corolla with ± 11 lobes, white above, brick red below; buds red. Fruit a twin berry, often only one half developing, shiny-black when ripe. Widely cultivated in gardens. Flowers heterostylous; all flowers on certain plants short-styled and on others long-styled. Fertilisation only takes place between flowers of different style-length, thus ensuring out-crossing. They are sweetly scented and pollinated by hawkmoths. *J. stenolobum* (mainly Mpumalanga and Northern Province) has hairy leaves.

Jo Onderstall

*Oenothera tetraptera

Onagraceae — Spring–Autumn

White evening primrose

Witaandblom

A low-growing perennial herb, with many stems from a woody taproot; covered with long hairs throughout; occurring as a weed in disturbed areas, often along roadsides. Leaves variously lobed and toothed, at least some in a basal rosette; margin often wavy. Flowers ± 60 mm in diameter; petals 4, at the end of a nectar-containing calyx tube, free, white fading to purplish pink. A native of Texas and Mexico. Flowers open just before sunset and last only a single night; pollinated by hawkmoths. Mature flower buds can be induced to open before one's eyes if enclosed by both hands in late afternoon. All ± 130 species of *Oenothera* (evening primroses) are native to North and South America. About 15 species naturalised as weeds in South Africa.

Braam van Wyk & Sasa Malan

21

Rogeria longiflora
Pedaliaceae   Summer–Autumn

White flower
Witblom

Robust, erect annual herb, up to 2 m high; occurring in semi-desert areas, often along roadsides. Leaves opposite, stalked, ovate, up to 300 mm long, Flowers in groups in axils of leaves; corolla tubular, with spreading lobes and a distinct basal spur, up to 80 mm long, white streaked with pink. Capsules ovoid, large (40–60 mm long), woody, with two spines towards base on dorsal side, dehiscent, many-seeded. Leaves unpleasantly scented. Dry remains of plants, with ripe (brown) capsules, may persist for several months; especially noticeable along roadsides. Seed roasted, ground, mixed with fat, and applied to wounds to stop bleeding and to relieve the pain from burns. Heated leaves are used as a poultice to heal cracked nipples on breastfeeding mothers.

Hester Steyn

Anemone fanninii
Ranunculaceae   Spring–Summer

Giant wild anemone
Grootanemoon

Robust perennial herb up to 1 m high, sprouting annually from a woody root-stock; occurring in grassland, usually in moist or rocky places. Leaves stalked, in a basal rosette, palmately 5–7-lobed, 250–350 mm in diameter, thick, hairy above and below; margin toothed, teeth often with reddish tips; stalk ± 700 mm long. Flowers in clusters of 2 or 3 at the end of a tall, erect stalk, fragrant; sepals petal-oid with indented tips, up to 70 mm long, white, often tinged pink; stamens numerous, with yellow anthers. Flowering is stimulated by veld fires; the new leaves mature after the plant has flowered. An infusion of the leaf is used as a purgative and to treat biliousness. Like many other grassland plants the giant wild anemone is difficult to grow in suburban gardens.

Pam Cooke

Clematis brachiata

Ranunculaceae   Summer–autumn

Traveller's joy

Klimop

An herbaceous or ± woody perennial vine, climbing vigorously by means of twining leaf stalks; occurring in wooded grassland and bushveld, usually in rocky places. Leaves opposite, 3–5-foliolate. Flowers solitary in leaf axils or in branched inflorescences at ends of stems, produced in abundance, sweetly scented; petal-like sepals white to pale cream, densely covered with hairs pressed close to the blade; stamens numerous and showy. Fruits numerous with long, silvery white, feathery styles. Very conspicuous along roadsides during autumn when fruiting plants form silvery white masses over woody vegetation. A tea made from the leaves is used to treat headaches, colds and chest ailments. Root and stem used as a remedy against syphilis and for a host of other ailments.

Braam van Wyk

Walafrida saxatilis

Scrophulariaceae   Summer

White-plume bush

Witaarbos

Perennial shrublet, up to 400 mm high with erect stems; occurring in karroid vegetation and grassland, often in deep, stony soils. Leaves in clusters, strap-shaped or ± needle-like, up to 4 × 0.8 mm; margin smooth. Flowers very small, in compact, 12–20 mm long panicles, each comprising many small spikes at the end of shoots; petals 5, irregular, with 2 facing up and 3 down, white; stamens and style exserted. Stem with its stiff spreading leaves resembles a pipe-cleaner. Unpalatable to livestock. Proliferates in deteriorating veld. Generic name commemorates Walafrid Strabo (809–849 AD), a medieval monk known as 'The squint', who wrote a book on gardening. About 36 species occur in the region; alternatively classified under Globulariaceae or Selaginaceae.

Bossie Kotzé

Thunbergia atriplicifolia

Acanthaceae Spring–Summer

Natal primrose

Grasveld-thunbergia

Perennial shrublet, up to 400 mm high with a tuberous rootstock and milky latex; occurring in grassland. Leaves ± stalkless, opposite, 20–60 × 10–35 mm, ± densely covered with soft hairs throughout; base rounded or heart-shaped. Flowers axillary, with 2 large overlapping bracts clasping the base; corolla pale cream with the inside of the tube pale yellow; stamens 4, with broad, flat filaments. Plants flower profusely after veld fires. Various parts used in traditional medicine. A hairwash is prepared from the leaf or unripe fruit. Differs from several other cream-flowered species of *Thunbergia* in the region in that it is not a twiner or scrambler. The genus forms a link between the Acanthaceae and Scrophulariaceae; often placed in a separate family, Thunbergiaceae.

Braam van Wyk & Sasa Malan

Asclepias fruticosa (= *Gomphocarpus fruticosus*)

Asclepiadaceae Spring–Summer

Milkweed

Melkbos

Evergreen perennial shrublet, up to 1.5 m high, with milky latex; occurring in grassland and bushveld, often in disturbed places. Leaves opposite, linear or linear-lanceolate. Flowers (see page 140) in axillary umbels, usually pendulous; corolla lobes reflexed, cream; corona with blunt tips, greenish. Fruit inflated, spindle-shaped, sparsely covered with bristle-like hairs. Stems contain a strong, silky bark fibre, formerly used for sewing. Used in traditional medicine to treat chest and stomach problems. Milky latex reportedly effective in the removal of warts. Seed hairs formerly used as tinder and to stuff pillows and mattresses. Larval food plant of the African monarch butterfly (*Danaus chrysippus*). Toxic substances derived from the plant are passed via pupa to adult insect for protection against predators.

Braam van Wyk

Leucadendron salignum

Proteaceae   Autumn–Spring

Common sunshine conebush

knoppiesgeelbos

A many-stemmed shrub, usually ± 1 m high, with a root-stock; occurring in fynbos, often in extensive stands. Leaves ± stalkless, 20–60 × 3–6 mm; base slightly twisted. Flowers small, yellowish or reddish, clustered in roundish heads, male and female ones on different plants; heads surrounded by showy yellow, cream or red involucral leaves, these being slightly longer than the foliage leaves. Female heads develop into globose, cone-like fruiting heads which stay on the plant until after a fire; they then open to release small, winged fruit. Female plants' tend to be smaller than males and are less branched with larger leaves; a difference perhaps due to the fact that females devote more resources for seed production. The more than 80 species of *Leucadendron* are all confined to South Africa, most occurring in the Cape Floristic Kingdom.

Leucospermum cuneiforme

Proteaceae   All year

Wart-stemmed pincushion

Gewone speldekussing

A many-stemmed shrub, up to 2 m high, arising from an underground root-stock; occurring in fynbos. Basal parts of old stems with warts and pustules. Leaves are stalkless, oblanceolate; tip rounded, with 3–10 glandular teeth. Flower heads are yellow, and made up of numerous flowers with long, colourful styles; the bracts are inconspicuous. While the flowers are still in bud the anthers deposit their pollen on a sticky swelling (pollen presenter) near the tip of the style. When the buds open, the perianth and stamens curl back to expose the long styles. This mechanism of pollen presentation ensures adequate transfer of pollen to pollinators, in this species mainly birds. The ± 48 species of pincushions are largely confined to South Africa; many are grown as cut flowers and garden ornamentals.

Colin Paterson-Jones

25

Didelta spinosa

Asteraceae　　　　　　　　Spring

Thorny salad bush

Doringslaaibos

Shrub or small, slender tree, up to 2.5 m high; occurring in semidesert areas, often in stony places. Leaves stalkless, ovate to elliptic, up to 70 × 60 mm, thick and ± succulent, usually hairless; apex often spine-tipped; margin usually with irregularly spaced, spine-tipped teeth. Flower heads (see page 140) solitary at ends of branches, radiate, ± 60 mm in diameter; ray and disc florets yellow; involucral bracts with the 5 outer ones leaf-like and spreading, the inner ones narrow and toothed. Heavily browsed by livestock, notably horses; taller plants often with a rounded crown above the browse line. Leaves used in salads, hence the common names. *D. carnosa*, a herbaceous shrublet from sandy areas along the west coast, has narrow leaves with the margins rolled under; leaves in some forms have white hairs.

Robert Archer

Euryops abrotanifolius

Asteraceae　　　　　　　Autumn–Spring

Resin bush

Geelmagriet

An erect perennial shrublet, up to 1 m high, single-stemmed or sparsely branched; occurring in fynbos, usually on sandy or rocky slopes. Leaves up to 90 mm long, pinnately divided into segments ± 1.5 mm wide, leathery. Flower heads (see page 140) on long, slender stalks, radiate, ± 50 mm in diameter, bright yellow; involucral bracts in one row, united to form a smooth cup. Plants often appear as pioneers after veld fires. A showy species often found on Table Mountain. More than 80 species of *Euryops* occur in the region, many with yellow flower heads on long, slender stalks above the foliage. Generic name derived from the Greek *eurys* = large and *ops* = eye, alluding to the showy flower heads. Several species grown in gardens. Plants need well-drained soil and full sun, and are tender to frost.

Braam van Wyk

*Flaveria bidentis

Asteraceae   All year

Smelter's bush
Smeltersbossie

Erect, leafy annual herb, up to 1 m high; occurring in bushveld, very common as a weed along roadsides and in disturbed places. Stems yellowish, hairless. Leaves opposite, with very short stalks, lanceolate to elliptic, up to 80 × 20 mm, with ± 3 prominent parallel veins; stalks of each leaf pair ± joined around the stem; margin toothed. Flower heads discoid (see page 140), with few flowers, yellow, arranged in dense terminal and axillary groups; involucral bracts 2–4, closely arranged in a single whorl to form a cylindrical tube. A native of tropical America. First recorded in South Africa in 1917. Probably introduced with fodder during the Anglo-Boer War, or as an impurity in bird seed. Easily controlled without herbicide by shallow cultivation or soil tilling during the seedling stage.

Braam van Wyk & Sasa Malan

Gazania krebsiana

Asteraceae   All year

Common gazania
Gewone botterblom

A low-growing annual or perennial herb, with milky latex; occurring in various vegetation types. Leaves in a basal rosette, long and narrow, greenish above, white-felted below; margin smooth, toothed or deeply lobed. Flower heads (see page 140) solitary, stalked, radiate, 30–80 mm in diameter; ray florets yellow, white, orange, red or shades of yellow and orange, often brownish at the base, with or without a whitish/black blotch; disc florets same colour as the outer portion of ray florets. A wide-ranging and extremely variable species, best subdivided into a number of taxa. Flowering in some forms stimulated by fire. Used for medicinal and magical purposes. Many showy cultivars are grown in gardens. Unfortunately not suited as cut flowers; heads open only in bright sunlight.

Braam van Wyk

Helichrysum decorum

Asteraceae   Summer–Autumn

Coastal yellow everlasting

Kusgeelsewejaartjie

Erect biennial or short-lived perennial herb, up to 1.3 m high; occurring in grassland or open bushveld, usually in coastal areas. Leaves on stems oblong-lanceolate or elliptic-lanceolate, up to 80 × 30 mm, upper surface cobwebbed, lower surface with greyish white, woolly hairs. Flower heads (see page 140) ± 30 mm in diameter, bright yellow, arranged in large, flat-topped panicles at the ends of stems. An attractive though little known garden plant. A number of very similar-looking, yellow-flowered species of *Helichrysum* occur in the region. *H. setosum* has sticky green leaves and flower heads solitary at the tips of long, leafy branchlets arranged in small flat-topped groups near ends of stems. *H. cooperi* has the flower heads arranged in well-branched, horizontally spreading panicles.

Helichrysum nudifolium

Asteraceae   Summer

Hottentot's tea

Hottentotstee

Erect perennial herb up to 1.3 m high; occurring in grassland and fynbos, often in dense stands. Leaves crowded near the base, linear-lanceolate to ± elliptic, the larger ones up to 600 × 300 mm, contracted to a stalk-like base, 3–7-veined, green and rough-textured above, white woolly below. Flower heads (see page 140) ± 3 mm in diameter, very many arranged in compact, ± flat-topped or rounded panicles at the ends of stems; involucral bracts in ± 6 rows, bluntly-pointed, pale or lemon yellow. A very common species in high-rainfall montane grassland. Leaves aromatic and used in traditional medicine to treat chest ailments, fevers, wounds and headaches. *H. coriaceum* has flower heads ± 5 mm in diameter, with straw-coloured involucral bracts. Common in Highveld grassland.

Braam van Wyk

Hirpicium bechuanense

Asteraceae   Summer

Botswana marigold

Botswana-gousblom

Annual or short-lived perennial herb, up to 400 mm high; occurring in bushveld, often alongside roads and in disturbed places. Leaves strap-shaped, grey-green above, white-felted below; margin toothed, with long bristly hairs towards base. Flowers (see page 140) solitary at ends of branches, radiate; ray florets yellow, with tips of petals 3-toothed; disc florets yellow; involucral bracts in 7 or 8 rows, ± united into a cup-like base with short, stiff hairs. Flowers open only in bright sunlight. Plants have proved experimentally to be toxic to sheep, with death occurring within two days. There are about eight species in the genus, all confined to southern and East Africa. They are readily distinguished from related groups by the involucral bracts and leaves, which are often covered by long, bristly hairs.

Braam van Wyk

Berkheya onopordifolia

Asteraceae   Summer

Tumbleweed berkheya

Tolbosdisseldoring

Bushy, short-lived perennial herb, up to 1 m high; occurring mainly in grassland and karroid vegetation. Leaves stiff and leathery, oblong, deeply pinnately lobed, up to 300 × 80 mm, green above, white-felted or with glandular hairs below; margin with coarse, triangular, spine-tipped teeth, interspersed with spines. Flower heads (see page 140) solitary or a few together at the ends of stems, radiate, up to 90 mm in diameter; ray and disc florets yellow; involucral bracts ± 10 mm wide, spine-tipped. After the fruiting heads have matured, the above-ground part of the plant dries out, breaks loose from the root and rolls about in the wind, thus distributing the seeds; dried plants often seen piled-up against fences along roadsides. Used in traditional medicine to treat feverish illnesses.

Braam van Wyk

Nidorella hottentotica

Asteraceae

Autumn–Winter

Hairy nidorella

Harige stinkkruid

An erect, sparsely branched annual or short-lived perennial herb, up to 1.5 m high; occurring in grassland and bushveld, often in disturbed places. Leaves strap-shaped, often ± undulating, densely covered with white, woolly hairs. Flower heads (see page 140) essentially discoid (ray florets very small, 2-lipped), arranged in ± flat-topped terminal groups, bright yellow. Inflorescences are visited by a wide range of insects. *N. auriculata* is common in KwaZulu-Natal and along the Eastern Transvaal Escarpment. It has hairy (though not whitish) leaves, with the veins prominent below and the base ± eared. *N. resedifolia*, a widespread weedy annual, has roughly hairy leaves that are often ± pinnately lobed. It is particularly common in North West, especially on old cultivated lands.

Braam van Wyk

Osteospermum sinuatum

Asteraceae

Winter–Spring

Karoo bietou

Karoobietou

Rounded, ± spreading perennial shrublet, up to 500 mm high and 1 m in diameter; occurring in karroid vegetation, often in large colonies. Leaves opposite, ovate to oblanceolate, 18–30 × 5–8 mm, semi-succulent, greyish green; margin widely toothed. Flower heads on short stalks at ends of stems, radiate, 25–35 mm in diameter; ray and disc florets yellow; involucral bracts in a single row, with membranous margins and a sharp tip. Fruit with large wings, borne in drooping fruiting heads. Plants are indicative of veld in good condition. Highly palatable to livestock; suitable for sowing into the veld to improve carrying capacity. Especially vulnerable to overgrazing during flowering and fruiting. Plants lose all or some of their leaves during unfavourable conditions.

John Manning

Pentzia globosa

Asteraceae   Summer

Grey karoo

Vaalkaroo

Rounded shrublet, up to 400 mm high; occurring in karroid vegetation and in grassland. Leaves alternate or in clusters, grey-green, 4–6 × 0.1–0.3 mm, 3-fid or ± pinnately lobed. Flower heads (see page 140) borne near the tips of branches, stalked, discoid, ± 6 mm in diameter, yellow. One of the most abundant bushes in the eastern parts of the Karoo; fairly unpalatable to livestock and often proliferating in overgrazed areas. The related *P. incana*, one of the dominant bushes in the Karoo, is of considerable economic importance as it is readily grazed by sheep and forms an important part of their diet. It has shorter (2–3 mm), undivided leaves. Also, some of the branches often curve downwards and root, thus anchoring them to the ground. Aromatic leaves impart a distinctive flavour to Karoo mutton.

Braam van Wyk

Senecio consanguineus

Asteraceae   Autumn–Spring

Starvation senecio

Hongerbos-senecio

Bushy annual herb, up to 1 m high, with a long taproot; most parts with sticky hairs; occurring in grassland, usually along watercourses and on rocky ridges, also very common as a weed on arable land. Leaves stalkless, strap-shaped, up to 50 × 20 mm; base ± eared, stem-clasping; margin sharply and coarsely toothed. Flower heads (see page 140) radiate; ray florets usually 6–8, yellow, reflexed with age; disc florets yellow; involucral bracts in one row, sticky. One of the few indigenous plant species that has become a troublesome weed; very conspicuous in maize fields during late winter, especially in North West. When fields are ploughed in late winter and spring the abundantly produced fluffy seeds may block the radiators of tractors, hence its other name *radiatorbossie* (radiator bush).

Ziets Zietsman

Senecio inornatus

Asteraceae

Summer

Tall marsh senecio

Groot vlei-senecio

A robust perennial herb, up to 2 m high, with a woody rootstock; occurring in grassland, usually in marshy places. Basal leaves long (± 600 × 50 mm) and elliptic, tapering to a long stalk at the base, often with traces of a white, woolly covering; margin ± toothed. Flower heads (see page 140) clustered in ± flat-topped inflorescences at the ends of tall, erect, flowering stems, radiate; ray florets 5, yellow, becoming reflexed at an early stage; disc florets yellow; involucral bracts ± 12. An easy-to-recognise species because of its tall flowering stems; often grows in dense stands. Root decoctions used in traditional medicine to treat palpitations, phthisis, coughs and difficult breathing, but such treatment is potentially dangerous; plants contain highly toxic alkaloids that may cause liver damage.

Braam van Wyk

Senecio latifolius

Asteraceae

Spring–Summer

Staggers bush

Dunsiektebossie

Robust, bluish green perennial herb, up to 1.5 m high, with a woody rootstock; occurring in grassland and bushveld, often in dense colonies. Stems 1 or 2, leafy throughout. Leaves elliptic, ± 90 × 40 mm, leathery; base ± heart-shaped; margin ± widely toothed. Flower heads (see page 140) in flat-topped groups at the ends of stems, radiate; ray florets usually 5, yellow; disc florets yellow. Readily recognised by its un-branched stems, which are ± uniformly leafy. Plants tend to proliferate in disturbed areas. One of the species responsible for *seneciosis*, one of the most significant plant poisonings of livestock in southern Africa. Chronic poisoning is known as Molteno straining disease in cattle and *dunsiekte* in horses. Toxins affect the liver. Widely used in traditional medicine.

Lorraine van Hooff

Senecio pleistocephalus

Asteraceae   Autumn–Winter

Bushveld canary creeper

Bosveldkanarieklimop

Robust, deciduous, succulent perennial creeper, usually clambering over woody vegetation; occurring in bushveld. Stems brittle. Leaves elliptic, glossy dark green, hairless; margin unevenly toothed. Flower heads (see page 140) in dense, flat-topped inflorescences, discoid; disc florets yellow, soon fading to brown; involucral bracts 5. A conspicuous plant in early winter when it brightens up the drab bushveld scenery; unfortunately the flowering period is very short. Flower heads are strongly honey scented; very popular with honeybees and other insects. Various parts used in traditional medicine. Closely related to *S. brachypodus*, a succulent creeper from forest margins in the Eastern Cape and KwaZulu-Natal. It has pungently scented, radiate flower heads, with 5–8 involucral bracts.

Braam van Wyk

Senecio polyanthemoides

Asteraceae   All year

Forest margin senecio

Woudrand-senecio

Sparsely branched, bushy annual herb, up to 1.8 m high; occurring along forest margins and in disturbed sites such as along roadsides, in old cultivated fields and felled plantations. Leaves lanceolate, up to 150 × 40 mm, upper surface glossy, dark green and hairless, lower surface white-felted; margin rolled under, toothed. Flower heads (see page 140) in terminal panicles, radiate; ray florets ± 8, yellow; disc florets yellow. Inflorescences visited by a wide range of insects. Introduced as a weed in the Cape Peninsula and Australia. Generic name based on the Latin *senex* = an old man; alluding to the fluffy, white, fruiting heads. One of the largest genera of flowering plants, comprising about 1 500 species, more than 300 reported from the region. Many are superficially very similar in appearance.

Braam van Wyk

33

Senecio tamoides

Asteraceae   Autumn–Winter

Canary creeper

Kanarieklimop

Robust, ± succulent perennial climber with twining stems; occurring along forest margins. Leaves ± triangular in outline, up to 80 x 80 mm, light green and glossy, usually hairless; margin unequally lobed; stalk up to 80 mm long. Flower heads (see page 140) in large, terminal clusters, radiate, up to 20 mm in diameter; ray florets usually 5, yellow; disc florets yellow; involucral bracts 6–8, ± 8 mm long, swollen at the base. A very showy species, widely cultivated as a climber in gardens. Plants must be supported by a trellis or allowed to twine into a tree. Stems root easily, but plants are sensitive to severe frost. They can be cut back after flowering, especially in colder areas where they tend to be semi-evergreen. Used in traditional medicine to treat certain human ailments and anthrax in cattle.

Senecio venosus

Asteraceae   Spring

Highveld senecio

Hoëveldse senecio

An erect perennial herb, up to 1 m high, with a woody rootstock; occurring in grassland and bushveld, often in rocky places. Leaves stalkless, lanceolate to oblong-lanceolate, up to 120 x 30 mm, blue-green, hairless, except for wool hidden deep in leaf axils; base heart-shaped; venation very conspicuous (translucent) when leaf is held up to the light. Flower heads (see page 140) numerous, in a spreading cluster at the end of a generally solitary, unbranched flowering stem, radiate or discoid; ray florets 5–7, yellow; disc florets yellow; involucral bracts ± 8, broad and flat. A very common species in Highveld grassland. Apparently not as acutely toxic to livestock as some of the other members of the genus. Powdered root used in traditional medicine as a snuff for the relief of headache.

Rhigozum obovatum

Bignoniaceae | Spring

Yellow pomegranate
Geelberggranaat

A rigid, compact shrub or small tree; occurring in karroid vegetation and valley bushveld, often in rocky places. Leaves opposite or in clusters, trifoliolate or simple, borne on short, spine-tipped side shoots; leaflets obovate, 5–13 x 2–5 mm, greyish green; apex tapering. Flowers in axillary clusters, showy, bright yellow. Fruit a flattened, pod-like capsule; seed with papery wings. Leaves and pods are heavily browsed by game and livestock, particularly goats; highly resistant to drought. *R. brevispinosum*, with a more northerly distribution, has leaves that are predominantly simple; root used medicinally to treat oedema. *R. zambesiacum*, from low-altitude bushveld, has pinnately compound leaves with 3–5 pairs of leaflets. All these species are mass bloomers with showy yellow flowers.

Photo credit: Piet van Wyk–Agfa

*Raphanus raphanistrum

Brassicaceae | Winter–Summer

Wild radish
Ramenas

An erect annual or biennial herb, up to 800 mm high: occurring as a weed on cultivated and fallow lands, also in other disturbed and often moist places. Basal leaves stalked, deeply pinnately lobed; stalk grooved. Flowers in axillary clusters; petals 4, free, distinctly stalked, yellow or rarely white, sometimes with dark veins. Fruit pod-like, erect, narrowly tapering, at least 4 times as long as they are wide, constricted between the seeds, eventually breaking at constrictions into 1-seeded portions. A native of Europe, now a common weed, particularly in wheat fields in the Western Cape and eastern Free State. Seed poisonous, potentially dangerous when harvested with wheat used for bread or animal fodder, one of the clinical signs being diarrhoea. Widely used in traditional medicine.

Photo credit: Braam van Wyk & Sasa Malan

*Caesalpinia decapetala

Caesalpiniaceae   Autumn–Spring

Mauritius thorn

Kraaldoring

Piet van Wyk–Agfa

Robust, evergreen, scrambling shrub or climber; invading forest margins, road-sides, watercourses and disturbed places, often forming dense, impenetrable thickets. Branchlets with numerous, randomly scattered, straight to hooked thorns. Leaves bipinnately compound; leaflets up to 8 mm wide. Flowers in elongated, erect, axillary racemes, pale yellow. Pods woody, flattened, sharply pointed at tip, indehiscent. A native of Asia; cultivated for security hedging and ornament. It is a declared weed in South Africa. Generic name commemorates Andreas Caesalpino (1519–1603), an Italian botanist and physician, often called the first plant taxonomist. His book, *De Plantis* (1583), classified about 1 500 species on the basis of several vegetative and floral characters.

Chamaecrista mimosoides (= *Cassia mimosoides*)

Caesalpiniaceae   Summer

Fishbone cassia

Visgraat-cassia

Braam van Wyk & Sasa Malan

Erect or prostrate annual or perennial herb, up to 500 mm high; occurring in grassland and bushveld. Leaves stalked, pinnately compound, with a ± circular gland on the stalk below the basal pair of leaflets; leaflets 35–65 pairs, ± 8 × 2 mm; axis with a long, narrow ridge along upper surface. Flowers in groups of 1–3 on internode above the leaf axil; petals yellow; sepals often tinged brownish or reddish. Pods dehiscent, splitting into two, spirally twisted valves. The leaflets are sensitive to touch; like most legumes they also fold closed at night. Used in traditional medicine to treat various skin conditions, dysentery and loss of appetite in children. The nine species of *Chamaecrista* in southern Africa have very similar flowers and are easily confused. Closely related to *Senna*, which has indehiscent pods.

Senna italica (= *Cassia italica*)

Caesalpiniaceae   Spring–Summer

Wild senna

Elandsertjie

Perennial herb, with trailing stems from a woody, black tap-root; occurring in grassland and bushveld, often along roadsides. Leaves pinnately compound; leaflets 10–35 × 10–25 mm, with rounded tips and small, finger-like glands in their axils. Flowers in stalked, axillary racemes; petals bright yellow. The sepals apparently secrete a nectary substance; they are actively visited by ants, the presence of which may protect the flowers against herbivorous insects. Seed used in traditional medicine and as a coffee substitute. Anthers have tiny apical pores; they must be vibrated at high frequency by bees to release the pollen. Forms are cultivated to provide some of the senna of commerce (dried leaflets and pods), a widely used purgative. Pods much preferred by eland, hence the Afrikaans common name.

Braam van Wyk

Cleome angustifolia

Capparaceae   Summer

Yellow mouse-whiskers

Geel-cleome

Slender, erect, blue-green annual herb, up to 1.5 m high; occurring in bush-veld, often in mopane veld and along roadsides. Stems smooth, occasionally with spindle-shaped swellings. Leaves palmately compound, with 3–10 leaflets; stalk up to 60 mm long. Flowers in lax, terminal racemes; petals 4, free, yellow, usually with a violet blotch at the base, the two lateral ones larger, 9–24 × 5–12 mm; stamens 8–18, the 2 or 4 fertile ones with filaments up to 40 mm long, incurved. Fruit a pod-like capsule. Following good rains plants may appear in large numbers. About 20 species of *Cleome* occur in the region. They usually have pink or yellow, spider-like flowers. In most of the region's other yellow-flowered species, all of the stamens are fertile. *C. gynandra*, with white flowers, is a popular vegetable.

Braam van Wyk

Commelina africana

Commelinaceae   Summer

Yellow commelina

Geeleendagsblom

Low-growing, hairless or hairy perennial herb with erect or trailing stems from a woody rootstock; occurring in grassland and bushveld, often on rocky outcrops. Leaves stalkless, long and narrow, flat or folded, forming a sheath at the base. Flowers borne in stalked, boat-shaped spathes; petals 3, the upper 2 well-developed and stalked, the lower one reduced and ± colourless. An extremely variable species; at least four varieties known in the region. Flowers open shortly after sunrise, fade before midday. Used in traditional medicine (especially root) to treat various ailments, including venereal disease, sterility as well as heart and bladder complaints. Young shoots and leaves are cooked as a green vegetable; ground peanuts may be added as a condiment.

Merremia palmata

Convolvulaceae   Summer

Finger-leaved merremia

Vingerblaar-merremia

Perennial herb, with long trailing or twining stems; hairless throughout; occurring in bushveld, often along roadsides. Leaves stalked, deeply palmately divided into 5–7 narrow (0.5–8 mm), finger-like lobes, up to 60 mm long. Flowers axillary, often solitary; corolla broadly funnel-shaped, 30–40 mm in diameter, cream to pale yellow with a deep maroon 'eye'; anthers cream, ± spirally twisted. Fruit a capsule, ± globose, dehiscent. The cream anthers are sharply contrasted against the dark corolla centre, undoubtedly a specialised adaptation to attract insect pollinators. *M. kentrocaulos*, a tall, ± woody climber with larger leaves (60–150 mm long and wide) and flowers (50–70 mm in diameter), is often seen along roads in the Kruger National Park and in Sekhukhuneland.

Braam van Wyk

Kalanchoe thyrsiflora

Crassulaceae   Autumn–Winter

White lady

Geelplakkie

Robust, erect succulent, up to 1.5 m high, most parts covered with a powdery whitish covering; occurring on rocky ridges in grassland and bushveld. Leaves stalkless, 80–120 × 30–70 mm, greyish green; margin smooth, often tinged with red. Flowers densely clustered towards the end of a tall, erect stem; corolla tube powdery whitish green outside, lobes spreading with upper surface deep yellow. Leaves in a basal rosette for one or more years, gathering enough resources to flower. Following the formation of the tall inflorescence, which takes place in a single season, the particular rosette dies; new ones may sprout from the rootstock. Although poisonous, used in traditional medicine as treatment against intestinal worms; plants are known to cause paralysis in livestock.

Martin von Fintel

Coccinia sessilifolia

Cucurbitaceae   Summer

Sessile-leaved cucumber

Muisvoëlkomkommer

Blue-green, herbaceous perennial climber, with tendrils and a tuberous rootstock; occurring in grassland and bushveld. Leaves stalkless, deeply palmately 5-lobed. Flowers axillary, male (illustrated) and female ones on separate plants; corolla pale cream to almost white, strongly veined. Fruit fleshy, pendulous, green mottled with white, ripening through yellow to red from the tip. Both fruit and tuber used as food by the San people in the Kalahari; the former is best when gathered green and cooked as a vegetable, the latter is roasted or boiled. Seed dispersal facilitated by birds, the seeds being removed as the fruit ripens from the tip. Fruit-eating birds are strongly attracted to red fruit, especially those that sequentially ripen from yellow, through orange and red, to purple-black.

Braam van Wyk & Sasa Malan

Braam van Wyk

Aspalathus hirta

Fabaceae   Spring

Spiny-leaved aspalathus
Stekelblaar-aspalathus

An erect, branched shrub, up to 2 m high; occurring in fynbos and renoster-veld. Stems short-haired to woolly. Leaves simple, needle-like, 5–12 mm long, rigid, green, hairless or almost so, sharply spine-tipped. Flowers (see page 140) solitary or in pairs on lateral short shoots or branches, pea-like; petals bright yellow, the standard with short hairs on the back. Pods ± 10 × 4 mm, densely woolly or silver-haired. With about 280 species, *Aspalathus* is the largest genus of flowering plants strictly confined to South Africa, the majority of species being associated with the Cape Fold Mountains in the winter-rainfall area. *A. linearis* is the source of rooibos tea, an important commercial crop. Grown mainly in the Clanwilliam District, it contains no caffeine and is popular as a health beverage.

Colin Paterson-Jones

Crotalaria laburnifolia

Fabaceae   Summer

Bushveld crotalaria
Bosveld-crotalaria

An erect, sparsely-branched annual herb, up to 600 mm high; occurring in bushveld, often along roadsides. Leaves trifoliolate; leaflets ± elliptic, hairless; stalk 40–90 mm long. Flowers (see page 140) in lax racemes, pea-like, yellow, often marked reddish brown. Pods inflated, often mottled with maroon when young. Although the toxicity of this species is not known, crotalarias have been associated world-wide with poisoning in animals; the plants contain toxic alkaloids responsible mainly for severe liver and/or lung damage in livestock. Locally, members of the genus have been associated with *jaag-siekte*, a chronic respiratory disease in horses and mules, and *stywe-siekte*, 'stiffsickness', in cattle, characterised by painful, warm hooves, and abnormal hoof growth during the chronic phase.

Braam van Wyk

Cyclopia intermedia

Fabaceae   Winter–Spring

Honeybush tea

Heuningbostee

Evergreen, rounded perennial shrublet, up to 1 m high; occurring in fynbos. Twigs golden brown. Leaves trifoliolate; leaflets elliptic. Flowers (see page 140) axillary, borne in clusters along the stems, pea-like, golden yellow, up to 15 mm long, honey-scented. Pods flat, brown, many-seeded. Resprouts after fire. Grown commercially. Leaves, twigs and flowers are cut into small pieces, allowed to ferment, dried, and used to make as a tasty tea with a honey-like flavour, hence the common names. The tea, which is caffeine-free, can be reboiled to give several servings before the flavour is lost. A strongly brewed tea is used in traditional medicine to treat various ailments, including coughs, colds and bladder problems. *C. subternata* is an erect, sparsely branched shrub; regenerates from seed after fire.

Ben-Erik van Wyk

Eriosema psoraleoides

Fabaceae   Summer

Shrubby yellow eriosema

Geelkeurtjie

A silvery green perennial shrublet, up to 2 m high; occurring in bushveld and grassland, often along roadsides. Branches strongly ribbed, with whitish hairs. Leaves trifoliolate, finely hairy above, densely silver haired below. Flowers (see page 140) in ± erect racemes of 10–50 flowers, pea-like, yellow. Pods compressed, ± 14 x 10 mm, 2-valved, hairy, dehiscent, 2-seeded. Flowers hang downwards when in bud, rise to the horizontal plane as they open, and return to their former position when they close. As the standard petal becomes fully reflexed, this forces the wing petals to turn from the vertical into the horizontal plane, thus acting as a landing platform for pollinators. Ripe seeds are cooked as a vegetable. Leaf and root widely used throughout tropical Africa in traditional medicine.

Braam van Wyk

Lebeckia cytisoides

Fabaceae   Winter–Summer   Common whistle-bush

Gewone fluitjiesbos

A silvery, densely-branched shrub, up to 2 m high; occurring in fynbos, often in rocky places. Leaves trifoliolate; leaflets narrowly elliptic, with a powdery grey coating; stalk up to 30 mm long. Flowers (see page 140) in short, loose racemes, pea-like, up to 20 mm long, bright yellow. Pods cylindrical, ± 25 x 2 mm. Genus characterised by the presence of two (instead of the usual one) bracts at the base of the flower stalk. A strip of bark obtained from a related species can be pressed into a split reed to form a whistle (Afrikaans: *fluitjie*), hence the common names. *L. spinescens*, an important grazing bush from the central Karoo, is a twiggy, low-growing shrublet with spinescent branchlets and solitary flowers. It shows a preference for sandy soils, hence its other common name, sandganna.

Liparia splendens

Fabaceae   All year   Mountain dahlia

Skaamblom

Spreading shrub, up to 2.5 m high; occurring in fynbos, usually on rocky mountain slopes. Leaves simple, oval, sharply pointed, 30–50 mm long, ± hairless, with 3 or more primary veins from the base of the blade. Flowers (see page 140) pea-like, arranged among prominent bracts in dense, drooping heads at the ends of curved branches; corolla with petals tightly overlapping, yellow flushed with orange. Pods compressed, 2-valved. The nodding flower heads have given rise to the Afrikaans common name (literally 'shy flower'). Adapted for pollination by sunbirds. Whilst the bird is probing the flower for nectar, the tip of the keel petal dusts pollen onto its head, or picks up pollen left by another plant. *Liparia*, a genus of about 20 species, is confined to the Cape Floristic Region.

Sebaea grandis

Gentianaceae   Summer

Large-flowered sebaea

Grootblom-sebaea

A slender, erect annual herb, up to 350 mm high; occurring in grassland, or in marshy places. Stems 4-angled. Leaves opposite, stalkless, lanceolate, ± 40 x 15 mm. Flowers terminal, solitary or few, ± 30 mm in diameter; petals 5, fused at the base, lobes spreading, pointed, cream or pale yellow; sepals with keel winged towards the base. Fruit a capsule, dehiscent, with many tiny seeds. An infusion of the plant is used as a love charm emetic and has a pleasant, but bitter taste. About 45 species of *Sebaea* occur in the region. Most have cream or yellow flowers, 1–3 tiny glands on the anthers and a swelling somewhere along the style. The corolla lobes are twisted in bud and the calyx segments keeled or winged. Genus named after Albert Seba (1665–1736), a Dutch naturalist and author.

Braam van Wyk & Sasa Malan

Sarcocaulon crassicaule

Geraniaceae   Winter–summer

Yellow bushman's candle

Geelboesmanskers

Fleshy, rigid, spiny, perennial shrublet, up to 500 mm high; occurring in semi-desert areas, usually in rocky places. Stems usually more than 10 mm in diameter. Leaves long- and short-stalked, obovate, usually 15 x 9 mm, with fine hairs; margin lobed, scalloped or toothed. Flowers solitary, axillary, up to 55 mm in diameter; petals 5, free, pale yellow. Leaves produced only after good rains; stalks persistent, hardened into spines. Bark with a thick, ± translucent outer covering impregnated with wax; inflammable and burns with a smoky flame, even in green plants, hence the common names. Waxy bark very effective in preventing water loss; a plant of *S. patersonii* remained alive for 11 years unplanted after removal from the ground. The ± 20 species of *Sarcocaulon* are all confined to southern Africa.

Braam van Wyk

Wachendorfia thyrsiflora

Haemodoraceae   Spring

Bloodroot

Rooiknol

Clump-forming perennial herb, up to 2 m high, with stem-tubers; occurring in fynbos, usually in swampy places. Leaves basal, in erect fans, ± 800 × 80 mm, conspicuously pleated along their length. Flowers in spike-like panicles at the ends of tall, erect stems; golden yellow. Plants have a 'left- or right-handed' floral structure, a mechanism promoting cross-pollination. In 'left-handed' flowers the style along with one of the three stamens is deflected to the left; a reverse situation exists in 'right-handed' ones. Grown as part of water features in gardens; dormant during summer, but may remain evergreen in cultivation. Tubers contain reddish pigments (arylphenalenones); also present in some other members of the family, but not found in any other organisms.

John Manning

Hypoxis hemerocallidea (= *H. rooperi*)

Hypoxidaceae   Spring–Summer

Hairy star-flower

Harigesterblom

Perennial herb, up to 400 mm high, with a vertical rhizome; occurring in grassland. Leaves appearing before the flowers, arranged in 3 ranks, rather stiff and broad (10–50 mm), arching outwards, covered with long hairs. Flowers 5–23, on one or more erect or spreading stems; perianth segments 6, bright yellow, hairy on the back. Flowers open in the morning, close by midday. Rhizome with yellow flesh, used in traditional medicine. Promoted by the popular press under the name 'African potato' as a 'miracle cure' for, amongst others, arthritis and prostate cancer. An anticancer compound has indeed been isolated from the plant. Also contains plant sterols, which have a proven beneficial effect on the immune system, but these are also present in fresh fruit and vegetables.

Braam van Wyk & Sasa Malan

Hypoxis rigidula

Silver-leaved star-flower

Hypoxidaceae Spring–Summer Silverblaar-sterblom

Perennial herb, usually with a single, stiffly erect shoot, up to 1 m high, with a fleshy, vertical rhizome; occurring in grassland. Leaves basal, ± erect, 500–1 400 x 3–15 mm, folded upwards along midrib, overlapping to form a stem-like base, with short and often silver hairs. Flowers ± 40 mm in diameter; perianth segments 6, bright yellow, hairy on the back. Being a vertical stem, the rhizome grows in length at the top; were it not for certain adaptations, it would soon emerge above ground. As in other members of the genus, the rhizome contains contractile roots. These roots can shorten considerably in length, thus pulling the rhizome down to maintain it at a particular level below the soil. In addition, the rhizome progressively dies at the bottom. Leaves used to make a strong rope.

Braam van Wyk & Sasa Malan

Bobartia orientalis

Common bobartia

Iridaceae Spring Gewone blombiesie

Rush-like, tussock-forming perennial herb, up to 1.3 m high, with a woody rhizome; occurring in fynbos, renosterveld and grassland. Leaves 2–8 per flowering stem, cylindrical, 1.2–2.5 mm in diameter, ± as long as stems. Flowers crowded in dense, ± globose heads at the ends of erect flowering stems, subtended by a usually green and erect spathe; perianth yellow with 6 segments, the outer ones 11–22 x 3.5–9 mm, inner ones slightly smaller, yellow. Grows in profusion in burnt areas; flowering stimulated by fire. Leaves very tough and avoided by livestock; plants proliferate and may become dominant in severely overgrazed veld. Leaves used for making brooms. *B. indica* has flexible leaves that are much longer than the flowering stems and larger outer perianth segments.

John Manning

Homeria pallida

Yellow tulp

Iridaceae   Spring–Summer   Geeltulp

Braam van Wyk & Sasa Malan

A slender, erect perennial herb, up to 500 mm high, with a corm; occurring in grassland and karroid vegetation, often on clayey soils in damp places. Leaf solitary, up to 1 m long, 5–15 mm wide, grooved. Flowers borne along an erect, unbranched or sparsely branched stem; perianth segments 6, spreading ± on the same plane, usually yellow, with brownish speckles at base; style branches flattened, petal-like. Leaves tough and fibrous, pleated when fresh to make whips and rope. Plants proliferate in overgrazed areas. Toxic to livestock in both fresh and dried state, the main toxic principles being bufadienolides. Death generally occurs 24 to 48 hours after ingestion of plants. Corms eaten with impunity by spring hares and pigs. *Homeria*, with ± 35 species, is confined to southern Africa.

Moraea fugax (= *M. edulis*)

Edible moraea

Iridaceae   Spring   Wituintjie

John Manning

Perennial herb, up to 400 mm high, with a corm; occurring in karroid areas and fynbos, usually in sandy places. Leaves 1 or 2, inserted high on the stem, immediately below the first branch, channelled, much longer than the stem, trailing. Flowers in a compact, branched inflorescence, iris-like, yellow, blue or white, strongly scented. Flowers very short-lived, lasting about half the day. Corms are edible, pleasant-tasting, and are used in many traditional recipes. An important food source for the first human inhabitants of the Western Cape. Wash corms to remove soil, cook in salty water till soft, remove from tunics and eat; or, transfer to boiling milk, add a little corn or maize meal, flavour with orange or naartjie peel. Also eaten by various animals such as porcupines, mole rats and baboons.

46

Moraea spathulata

Iridaceae   All year

Large yellow moraea

Grootgeeltulp

An erect, usually clump-forming perennial herb, up to 900 mm high, with a corm; occurring in open grassland, often in rocky places. Leaf solitary, ± flat above, up to 1 m × 15 mm, straggling, usually dried at the tip. Flowers borne near the ends of tall, erect stems, iris-like; perianth segments yellow, with deep-yellow nectar guides at the base of the outer tepals. Plants in different geographical areas have very variable flowering times. An attractive and easily grown garden plant, even in areas with mild frost. Leaves fibrous; used to make rope. Poisonous to livestock. *M. alticola*, the largest and most robust species in the genus, is found above 2 200 m in the Drakensberg. It has the basal parts surrounded by coarse, fibrous tunics and the flowers are pale yellow.

Martin von Fintel

Bulbine latifolia

Liliaceae   Spring

Broad-leaved bulbine

Rooiwortel

Succulent perennial, up to 1 m high; aloe-like, but without thorns; occurring in karroid vegetation and valley bushveld. Leaves in a basal rosette, ± 300 × 80 mm, thick and fleshy, dull green, the tapering tips often recurved (± wilted). Flowers in long racemes at the ends of erect, unbranched stalks, yellow, with bearded filaments. Fruit a capsule, globose, splitting open with 3 valves. Sap used in traditional medicine to treat skin disorders (see next species), whereas an infusion or brandy tincture of the dried root is taken internally for a variety of ailments, including diabetes, rheumatism, urinary complaints and blood disorders. Very similar to *B. natalensis* (with which it may well be conspecific), a species extending from the Eastern Cape through KwaZulu-Natal to the Mpumalanga Escarpment.

Braam van Wyk

47

Bulbine narcissifolia

Liliaceae | Spring–Summer

Strap-leaved bulbine

Wildekopieva

An erect perennial herb, up to 300 mm high, with a short rootstock and fleshy roots; occurring in grassland, often in large colonies. Leaves in a basal rosette, ± erect, flattened, 5–20 mm wide, greyish green, ± fleshy. Flowers numerous, densely clustered at the end of a long, sturdy, erect stalk, yellow; filaments with long, yellow hairs. Fruit a capsule, 3-locular; many seeds per locule. Plants may proliferate in overgrazed areas. The leaves contain a yellowish sap that is a popular traditional first-aid remedy. Sap is applied directly from a freshly broken leaf onto burns, sunburned skin, rashes, cold sores, insect bites and minor cuts and scrapes. Several other members of the genus, all easily recognised by their yellow flowers and bearded filaments, are used in a similar manner.

Braam van Wyk & Sasa Malan

Bulbinella latifolia

Liliaceae | Spring

Broad-leaved cat's tail

Breëblaarkatstert

Sturdy, erect perennial herb, up to 1 m high, with a fibrous, erect rhizome; occurring in karroid vegetation and fynbos, often forming large stands in seasonally damp areas. Leaves tapering, channelled, up to 500 × 65 mm. Flowers small (6–8 mm in diameter), densely clustered in cylindrical racemes on tall inflorescence stalks, yellow (var. *latifolia*) or rarely orange (var. *doleritica*; which is confined to the Nieuwoudtville area). Fruit a capsule, 3-locular; seeds 1 or 2 per locule. May be confused with *B. nutans*, which has much narrower (± 10 mm) leaves and broader (± 50 mm), conical racemes. The genus has a widely disjunct distribution; 17 species in the winter-rainfall area of the region; six in New Zealand. Distinguished from similar-looking bulbines by its hairless filaments in the flower.

John Manning

Kniphofia porphyrantha

Liliaceae   Spring–Summer

Highveld red-hot poker

Hoëveldvuurpyl

An erect perennial herb, up to 1 m high, with fibrous roots; occurring in grassland, usually in marshy places and in dense groups. Leaves basal, ± flat above, at first erect, later arching, yellow-green; margin smooth. Flowers crowded into dense, spike-like inflorescences borne well above the leaves, tubular and ± drooping, orange when in bud, lemon yellow when open. Used in traditional medicine to treat female ailments. Easily confused with several other similar-looking species; more than 50 species of *Kniphofia* occur in the region. *K. ensifolia* is a robust Highveld species with a distribution mainly west of the Drakensberg Escarpment, extending to the Northern Cape and western Free State. Its open flowers are pale yellow or greenish white.

Braam van Wyk

Monopsis lutea

Lobeliaceae   Summer

Yellow monopsis

Geel-monopsis

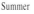

Perennial herb, with creeping or straggling stems, up to 300 mm high; occurring in fynbos and coastal vegetation, invariably in damp places such as seepage areas or along streams. Leaves alternate, narrow; margin toothed. Flowers solitary, axillary or terminal, 2-lipped, with 3 petals bent upwards and two downwards, ± 20 mm in diameter, bright yellow; corolla tube concealing the staminal tube and style, split to the base between the 2 lower lobes. Generic name derived from the Greek *monos* = one and *opsis* = appearance, probably alluding to the corolla, which is almost regular in some species; specific name from the Latin *luteus* = deep yellow. Related to *Lobelia*, which usually has a blue or purple 2-lipped corolla with the 3-lobed lip facing downwards.

John Manning

Gossypium herbaceum

Malvaceae — Summer–Autumn

Wild cotton

Wildekatoen

Straggly perennial shrub or scrambler, up to 2 m high; occurring in hot, frost-free, low-altitude bushveld (common in mopane veld). Leaves stalked, alternate, ± rounded in outline, deeply 5–7-lobed, heart-shaped at the base. Flowers solitary in leaf axils; lower calyx whorl of 3 leaf-like segments, with deeply incised margins; upper calyx whorl short, cup-shaped; petals 5, free, bright yellow, with a dark maroon centre, fading to orange. Fruit a capsule, 15–20 mm in diameter, dehiscent; seeds covered with white cotton wool. Plants are particularly conspicuous during the fruiting stage. Cotton from seed used by birds for lining their nests. Distant relative (even parent) of cultivated cotton (mainly cultivars of *G. hirsutum*), the most important natural fibre in the world today.

Braam van Wyk

Hibiscus calophyllus

Malvaceae — Summer

Wild stockrose

Wildestokroos

Shrubby perennial herb, up to 2 m high; occurring in bushveld and riverine bush, often in shady or moist places. Leaves ± circular, rarely 3–5-lobed, up to 120 mm in diameter, velvety; base heart-shaped; margin toothed; stalk up to 50 mm long. Flowers solitary in leaf axils, up to 120 mm in diameter, yellow with a dark maroon centre; lower calyx whorl of 5 segments, relatively broad in the middle, tapering to a long, hair-like tip; upper calyx whorl with lobes ovate to ovate-lanceolate, usually 3-veined, joined to nearly halfway. About 55 species of *Hibiscus* occur in the region. In *H. lunarifolius* the lower calyx segments are usually broadest near the base and the flowers lack a dark centre. *H. engleri* has 3–5-lobed leaves, hairs which create extreme irritation and a lower calyx of 7–10 segments.

Braam van Wyk & Sasa Malan

Hibiscus cannabinus

Malvaceae   Summer

Kenaf
Kenaf

Braam van Wyk

Erect annual herb, up to 2 m high; stems with scattered, often purplish prickles; occurring in bushveld, often as a weed in cultivated lands or other disturbed places. Leaves ± rounded in outline, 3–7-lobed, up to 150 mm in diameter, with a few minute prickles on the veins; margin toothed; stalk up to 22 mm long, with prominent nectar-secreting gland on the under surface near the base of the midrib (visited by ants). Flowers solitary, axillary, or in terminal racemes, up to 100 mm in diameter, pale yellow or cream with a very dark purple centre. Commercially grown for its strong jute-like bark fibre ('kenaf' or 'Deccan hemp'), especially in India and southeastern Europe. Leaves, flowers and young fruit cooked as a green vegetable. Seed oil used medicinally and in oil lamps.

Conicosia pugioniformis

Mesembryanthemaceae   Spring

Large pigsroot
Gansies

Wayne Matthews

Sprawling perennial or biennial succulent, up to 400 mm high, with a taproot; occurring in strandveld and karroid vegetation, usually in deep sand or disturbed places. Leaves opposite, elongated, ± 3-sided. Flowers solitary, on stout stalks, ± 100 mm in diameter, unpleasantly scented; petals thread-like, numerous, arranged in several whorls, yellow. Capsules large, cone-shaped, with 12 or more chambers. Flowers open in the afternoon and close at sunset; often visited by beetles. The capsules are unusual among mesembs in that the valves open under dry conditions to release the seed. In most other groups the capsules are closed when dry and open when wet. Naturalised as a weed in parts of Australia. *C. elongata*, the only other species, has tuberous roots and cylindrical leaves.

51

*Oenothera jamesii
Onagraceae   Spring–Summer

Giant evening primrose
Reuse aandblom

Erect, branched, herbaceous perennial, up to 2 m high; occurring in moist, disturbed places, often along roadsides. Leaves alternate, broadly lanceolate to elliptical, ± stalkless; margin shallowly toothed. Flowers solitary in leaf axils, up to 80 mm in diameter, with a calyx tube 60–100 mm long; petals 4, bright yellow, fading to pinkish. Capsules ± cylindrical, ± 25 × 10 mm, dehiscent, with numerous tiny seeds. A native of North America. Evening-primrose oil, a rich source of gammalinolenic acid, is extracted from the seed of members of the genus. It is used against arthritis and many other ailments, notably premenstrual tension and atopic eczema. It is also extensively used in cosmetic skin products and as a dietary supplement. Seed of some species still viable after 80 years.

Disa woodii
Orchidaceae   Winter–Spring

Wood's disa
Wood-se-disa

Stout, unbranched, erect perennial herb, up to 700 mm high, with a tuber, occurring in grassland, usually in damp and marshy places, also on roadside embankments. Leaves sheathing at the base, extending up the stem, ± fleshy. Flowers small, crowded in an elongated, cylindrical, terminal spike, bright yellow; outer 3 petal-like sepals 5–7 mm long, the dorsal one with a slender spur ± 1.5 mm long. Plants usually grow in large colonies and are visible from afar. Orchids have a complicated floral structure; the single stamen has become united with the style and stigma to form a structure called the column. Pollen grouped into masses (pollinia). *D. chrysostachya*'s flowers are more orange in colour, and the spur inflated and much longer than the dorsal sepal. *D. polygonoides* has bright red flowers.

Braam van Wyk

Braam van Wyk & Sasa Malan

Eulophia angolensis (= *Lissochilus buchanani*)

Tall marsh orchid

Orchidaceae	Summer	Reuse vlei-orgidee

Robust, erect perennial herb, up to 2 m high, with a tuberous rhizome; occurring in grassland, invariably in marshy places. Leaves basal, stiffly erect, up to 900 x 50 mm, longitudinally pleated. Flowers in terminal racemes, bright lemon-yellow, pleasantly scented; sepals petal-like, 3, erect, sometimes tinged olive and purplish brown; lower petal (lip) with 3–5 narrow ridges and a short basal pouch (spur), partly covered by the two lateral petals. Plants often grow in large colonies and are a spectacular sight with their tall inflorescences that stand well above the marsh vegetation. The inflorescence is produced next to the leaf-bearing shoot. Rhizome infusions are taken as love charm emetics by young Zulu men. About 42 species of *Eulophia* are native to the region.

Braam van Wyk

Oxalis pes-caprae

Yellow sorrel

Oxalidaceae	Autumn–Spring	Langbeensuring

Perennial herb, up to 400 mm high, with or without a naked stem below the leaves, with a tuberous bulb; occurring in semidesert vegetation and fynbos, often among rocks or as a weed of cultivation. Leaves in a rosette, trifoliolate; leaflets wedge-shaped, deeply lobed at the tip; stalk up to 120 mm long. Flowers in heads of 3–20 at the ends of tall, ± erect stalks, drooping in bud; corolla broadly funnel-shaped, with 5 petals, yellow; sepals often tipped with orange warts. Leaves and flowers are cooked, mixed with goats' milk when cold, strained and served as a tasty beverage. Used in many other traditional recipes; bulbs also edible. An introduced weed in many parts of the world, especially troublesome in Australia. Grazed in large quantities, plants may cause oxalic-acid poisoning in sheep.

Braam van Wyk

*Argemone ochroleuca (= *A. subfusiformis*)   White Mexican poppy

Papaveraceae   Spring–Summer   Bloudissel

Blue-green, spiny annual herb, up to 1 m high, with a distinctive unpleasant odour when crushed; occurring throughout the region as a weed of disturbed places. Leaves stalkless, deeply pinnately lobed; margin toothed, teeth ending in hard, yellowish spines. Flowers solitary, terminal, ± 50 mm in diameter; petals pale cream to almost white; stamens many, yellow. Fruit a spiny capsule, dehiscent. A native of Mexico, now a cosmopolitan weed. Often a pioneer on bare ground, thus preventing soil erosion. Spiny fruit and leaf-lobes may contaminate wool. Plants contain a yellow milky latex and toxic alkaloids. *A. mexicana*, also a weed from tropical America, has thin-textured green leaves and bright yellow flowers. It has a more restricted distribution along the east coast.

Ranunculus baurii   Large-leaved buttercup

Ranunculaceae   Summer   Grootblaarrenonkel

Perennial herb, up to 1.2 m high, with a rootstock; occurring in grassland and along forest margins, usually in wet places. Leaves roundish, 50–200 mm in diameter; veins whitish on upper surface; margin closely and bluntly toothed, red; stalk attached to centre of blade, 100–450 mm long, hollow. Flowers solitary in small plants, many in branched inflorescences in large plants; petals 13–15, shiny yellow; stamens numerous. Characteristic species of the high Drakensberg; leaf size diminishes with altitude. The genus is known for its toxic compounds, although nothing appears to be published on the chemistry of this species. Generic name comes from the Latin *rana* = frog, as many members grow in wet places where frogs abound. Seven species occur in the region.

Grielum humifusum

Rosaceae Spring

Common grielum
Pietsnot

Prostrate annual herb, with creeping stems radiating from a fleshy taproot; occurring on sandy soils in karroid vegetation and strandveld, often along roadsides and in disturbed areas. Leaves divided into broad segments, with fine woolly hairs below. Flowers produced in abundance, 20–30 mm in diameter, shiny lemon yellow, with a white ring in the centre. A showy component of the spectacular mass flowering spring displays in Namaqualand and elsewhere in the Western Cape. Flowers opening in bright sunshine. The fleshy roots are very slimy, hence the Afrikaans common name; it is a favourite food of the duiker and was formerly also extensively used as food by humans. *G. grandiflorum* has finely divided leaves with silvery hairs, and shiny dark yellow flowers with a green centre.

Gerald Cubitt

Hermannia cuneifolia

Sterculiaceae Winter–spring

Yellow healing-bush
Geelpleisterbos

A spreading, much-branched, perennial shrublet, up to 1 m high; occurring in karroid vegetation and fynbos. Leaves in tufts, wedge-shaped, 3–5 × 1–3 mm, densely covered with star-shaped hairs on both surfaces; margin coarsely toothed. Flowers in spike-like groups at ends of shoots, drooping, sweetly scented; petals 5, spirally twisted, 6–10 mm long, yellow, fading to orange. Once pollinated, the yellow flowers change to orange. This signals to pollinating insects which flowers still require their services. Palatable to livestock and drought resistant. Decoctions and infusions of the aromatic leaves are used in traditional medicine to treat sores; also taken internally for various ailments, hence the common names. Generic name after Paul Hermann (1640–1695), one of the first plant collectors at the Cape.

Bossie Kotzé

Gnidia capitata

Thymelaeaceae — Spring

Curry flower — Kerrieblom

Herbaceous perennial shrublet, up to 500 mm high, with a tuberous rootstock; occurring in grassland. Stems reddish brown. Leaves stalkless, narrowly elliptic, ± 30 × 6 mm, sharply pointed, often bluish green, ± hairless. Flowers in lax, few-flowered heads, without a prominently elongated subtending stalk; sepals 5, petal-like, mustard-yellow; petals small, scale-like. Flowering stimulated by veld fires; a typical pre-rain flower of the Grassland Biome. Used as a snuff to treat headaches; also utilised for magical purposes. Often associated with, and flowering at the same time as *G. caffra*, a species characterised by sparsely hairy leaves, and lemon-yellow flowers. Common names allude to the floral colour. About 100 species of *Gnidia* occur in the region; all have a very tough bark.

Braam van Wyk & Sasa Malan

Gnidia kraussiana

Thymelaeaceae — Spring

Lesser yellow head — Harige gifbossie

Perennial shrublet, up to 500 mm high, with annual shoots from a fleshy tuber; occurring in grassland. Stems robust, hairy. Leaves elliptic, ± 30 × 10 mm, sharply pointed, sparsely to densely hairy; margin often fringed with hairs; stalk up to 2 mm long. Flowers in compact heads of 18–35 flowers, the latter carried on a prominently elongated leafless stalk; sepals petal-like, yellow; petals scale-like. Flowering stimulated by veld fires in late winter. Plants are highly toxic and have been used as a fish and arrow poison; contains poisonous substances known to cause skin tumours. Decoctions of the tuber are nevertheless widely employed to treat a variety of ailments. Also used as a medicine to heal fractured limbs in livestock; injected by means of a hollow reed into the limb near the fracture.

Braam van Wyk & Sasa Malan

Lippia scaberrima

		Makwassie bush
Verbenaceae	Summer	Makwassiebossie

Braam van Wyk

Rounded shrublet, up to 600 mm high, with annual shoots from a woody rootstock; occurring in grassland and bushveld. Leaves opposite, ± elliptic, coarsely hairy; margin toothed. Flowers very small, cream, densely clustered in rounded or usually elongated axillary racemes; bracts prominent, green. Crushed plants are strongly and pleasantly ± mint-scented. An infusion of the leaves is widely used as a herbal tea to treat various ailments, with proven efficiency when used as a mouth-wash against gum infections. North West town of Makwassie named after original San name for this species. Four species of *Lippia* occur in the region, all highly aromatic. *L. rehmannii* is a small, lemon-scented shrublet. *L. javanica*, an erect, ± woody shrub up to 2 m high, is common in high-rainfall bushveld and grassland areas.

Sisyndite spartea

		Desert broom
Zygophyllaceae	Spring–Summer	Woestynbesem

Robert Archer

Many-branched shrub, up to 2.5 m high, with grey-green twigs; occurring in semidesert areas, often on rocky outcrops or along dry watercourses. Leaves compound, ± opposite, 70–300 mm long; leaflets obovate, tiny (20 x 8 mm). Flowers usually solitary in forks of branches, cup-shaped; petals 5, broadly obovate, yellow, with orange-yellow lines. Seed capsules with long, fluffy, cream hairs. What appear to be leaves are in fact leaflets (they lack axillary buds); terminal branchlets are the main axes of pinnate leaves. The only member of the genus; restricted to the Northern Cape and southern Namibia. Flowers close at night, often providing a shelter for the males of one of its pollinators, the long-tongued solitary bee (*Parafidelia pallidula*), which do not have burrows of their own.

Ziets Zietsman

Tribulus terrestris

Zygophyllaceae Summer

Devil's thorn

Dubbeltjie

Braam van Wyk

Annual herb, with much-branched creeping shoots; widespread, often a weed in disturbed areas. Leaves opposite, usually with one of a pair shorter than the other, pinnately compound, without a terminal leaflet. Flowers solitary in leaf axils, 6–10 mm in diameter; petals 5; stamens 10; pistil with style absent. Fruit woody, with sharp spines. A common indigenous weed. Flowers open after sunrise and close by midday. Despite being highly nutritious to livestock, the plant is at times the cause of a major hepatogenous photosensitivity disease in sheep, known as *geeldikkop*, 'yellow thick head'. Outbreaks of the disease usually occur sporadically when wilted plants are grazed during hot, dry spells following summer rains, especially in the Karoo. Ostrich eat the spiny fruit with impunity.

Zygophyllum morgsana

Zygophyllaceae Winter–Spring

Tortoise bush

Skilpadbos

John Manning

Colin Paterson-Jones

Robust perennial shrub, up to 1.5 m high; occurring in karroid vegetation and fynbos, especially common in strandveld. Branches covered with lichens in areas with high incidence of fog. Leaves bifoliolate, ± succulent; leaflets obovate; stalk 12–25 mm long. Flowers in pairs at the ends of branches; petals 4, free, pale yellow, with a dark purplish blotch at the base. Fruit pendulous, with 4 prominent, membranous wings. Crushed leaves are unpleasantly scented; apparently toxic and the cause of diarrhoea in livestock. Powdered seeds are used as an old Cape remedy for convulsions, paralyses and 'strokes'. More than 50 species of *Zygophyllum* occur in South Africa. The group is easily recognised by the bifoliolate leaves. Some species are important grazing plants in the arid parts of the region.

Thunbergia alata

Acanthaceae — Summer

Black-eyed Susan
Swartoognooi

Braam van Wyk

Herbaceous creeper, with slender, annual twining stems which sprout from a perennial root system; occurring along forest margins and in bushy places. Leaves hairy; base heart-shaped; petioles winged. Flowers on slender stalks and subtended by two small, leaf-like bracts, trumpet-shaped, bright orange, with inner surface of the tube dark, purplish black. Attractive garden plant; quick growing and self-seeding, often treated as an annual. Genus name commemorates the Swedish botanist, Carl Peter Thunberg (1743–1828), one of Linnaeus' pupils and often described as the 'father of Cape botany'. His famous book, *Flora Capensis* (1823), contains the results of three years (1772–1775) of travelling and botanical collecting in the region, including the description of many plant species new to science.

Clivia caulescens

Amaryllidaceae — Spring–Summer

Escarp bush lily
Eskarp-boslelie

Braam van Wyk

Evergreen perennial herb, up to 1 m high, with creeping rhizomes; occurring in moist, humus-rich places in the shade of forest or large boulders, sometimes growing on trees or rocks. Leaves strap-shaped, 300–400 × 30 mm, dark green. Flowers in umbels on erect stalks, tubular, drooping, deep orange to red, with a yellowish green tip. Fruit a berry, red. A shade-loving species, widely cultivated in gardens. It is characterised by a length of thick stem above ground, which bears the leaves. Extensive stands may be seen in the 'rain-forest' at the God's Window look-out along the Drakensberg Escarpment near Graskop in Mpumalanga. Very similar to *C. gardenii* and *C. nobilis*, by which it is replaced further south in the forests of KwaZulu-Natal and the Eastern Cape.

Clivia miniata

Amaryllidaceae   Spring

Bush lily
Boslelie

Evergreen perennial herb, up to 1 m high, with creeping rhizomes; occurring in moist places in the shade of forest, often growing on rocks. Leaves strap-shaped, 300–400 × 30 mm. Flowers in umbels on erect stalks, bell-shaped, spreading, orange with a whitish-yellow centre. All four species of *Clivia* are confined to southern Africa. This species has the most spectacular flowers. An extremely popular garden or pot plant for shady situations; extensively cultivated worldwide. A cool winter stimulates flowering. Cultivars include forms with bright yellow, whitish, dark orange-red and bicoloured flowers. Although rhizomes of all bush lilies contain alkaloids and are extremely toxic, plants of this species, as well as *C. nobilis*, are widely used in traditional medicine.

Braam van Wyk

Arctotis fastuosa (= *Venidium fastuosum*)

Asteraceae   Winter–Spring

Bitter marigold
Bittergousblom

Annual herb, up to 600 mm high; occurring in semidesert areas, often in profusion on sandy soils. Leaves deeply-lobed, up to 150 mm long, sparsely covered with white, woolly hairs. Flower heads (see page 140) up to 60 mm in diameter, borne singly on an erect leafy stalk; ray florets arranged in two series, orange in colour, those of the inner series with a conspicuous dark brown to black blotch at the base; disc floret black in bud, yellow when open; involucral bracts covered in a white wool. As one of about 66 species of *Arctotis* in southern Africa, this species, with its large, brilliant flowers, creates spectacular spring shows in Namaqualand; it is often grown in gardens. Common names refer to the bitter taste imparted to the milk of cattle that have grazed on the plants.

John Manning

Dimorphotheca sinuata

Asteraceae   Winter–Spring

Namaqualand daisy

Namaqualandse madeliefie

Sprawling annual herb; occurring in semidesert areas, particularly on disturbed and sandy sites. Leaves simple, hairless; margin shallowly toothed. Flower heads (see page 140) solitary, up to 80 mm in diameter; ray florets in a single series, orange-yellow. Prominent constituents of the brilliant orange mass displays of spring flowers in Namaqualand. Flowers only open fully in bright sunshine. Seeds of disc florets flat and thin-walled with papery wings. They are rather fragile and germinate readily the next rainy season. Seeds of ray florets elongated with thick, hard walls. These thick-walled seeds may remain dormant for several years, thus providing protection against drought, which seedlings of the mass germinating thin-walled seeds seldom survive. Cultivated in gardens and parks worldwide.

Roger de la Harpe

Gorteria diffusa

Asteraceae   Winter–Spring

Beetle daisy

Kewermadeliefie

Sprawling annual herb, up to 300 mm high; occurring in semidesert areas, often in dense stands. Leaves usually unlobed, roughly hairy above, white-felted below. Flower heads (see page 140) borne singly on erect stalks, 20–35 mm in diameter; ray florets deep orange above, purplish below, two or more with a conspicuous black and dark brown blotch, usually marked with green and white dots towards the base; disc florets yellow; involucral bracts long and spiny. The peculiar dark markings on the ray florets mimic certain beetles. The role of the markings is believed to be to attract specific beetle pollinators, and/or to repel destructive beetles. Another suggestion is that these black spots serve to attract a bee fly pollinator, *Megapalpus nitidus*, through visual sexual mimicry.

John Manning

Ursinia calenduliflora

Asteraceae   Winter–Spring

Mountain marigold

Bergmagriet

Annual herb, up to 360 mm high; occurring in semi-desert areas, often in dense stands on sandy soils and fallow fields. Leaves up to 50 mm long, finely divided into narrow segments. Flower heads (see page 140) borne solitary on slender, erect stalks, drooping when young, 20–50 mm in diameter; ray florets orange, usually with a purple base; disc florets yellow; involucral bracts in many rows, with conspicuous transparent tips. Fruit tipped by white, petal-like scales. One of the many species of orange and yellow daisies which, following good winter rains, covers the fields and mountains of the usually drab semidesert Namaqualand with a blanket of colour. There are about 35 species of *Ursinia* in the region; at least 14 occur in Namaqualand, with *U. cakilefolia* often abundant on fallow land.

Gretel van Rooyen

Begonia sutherlandii

Begoniaceae   Spring–Summer

Wild orange begonia

Oranje-wildebegonia

Soft perennial herb, up to 1 m high, with one or several somewhat fleshy stems from a small tuber; occurring mainly in shady and rocky places in forest, often forming large colonies, sometimes epiphytic on trees. Stems green, tinged red. Leaves thin-textured, up to 250 × 150 mm, with a satiny sheen above; base asymmetrical; margin sharply toothed, frequently lobed as well. Flowers in axillary or terminal, many-flowered inflorescences, pale to deep orange. Fruit 3-winged. One of the most widespread of the African begonias, ranging from central through East Africa as far south as the Eastern Cape. As in other begonias, male and female flowers are borne separately, but on the same plant. Leaf and stem infusions are used to treat heartburn and other ailments.

Lorraine van Hooff

Tecomaria capensis (= *Tecoma capensis*)

Bignoniaceae   All year

Cape honeysuckle

Kaapse kanferfoelie

Many-stemmed climbing shrub or, rarely, a small tree to 4 m high; occurring in bushveld, thicket and along forest margins. Leaves opposite, pinnately compound. Leaflets with small hair tufts in axils of principal side veins below; margin scalloped or toothed. Flowers in terminal racemes, orange-red. Capsules pod-like, up to 130 mm long, splitting to release many papery-winged seeds. Sunbirds feast on the abundant nectar in the flower and also act as pollinators. The stigma is touch-sensitive, with the two lobes folding together when touched. Bark used medicinally. Widely cultivated as a garden ornamental, with many cultivars, including forms with yellow, red, pink and pale orange flowers. Related to the South and Central American genus *Tecoma*, some of which are hummingbird-pollinated.

Braam van Wyk

Crocosmia mathewsiana

Iridaceae   Summer

Mathews' crocosmia

Mathews-se-valentynsblom

Erect, deciduous perennial, up to 1.8 m high, with a corm; occurring in grassland, usually along the banks of mountain streams, in full sun or semishade. Leaves arranged in a fan, sword-shaped, usually more than 30 mm wide. Flowers in a large, erect, laxly branched panicle, all pointing to one side; perianth bright reddish orange, tepals spreading; stamens with only anthers exserted from perianth tube. A stunning plant. Threatened by commercial afforestation. Resembles *C. masonorum* from the Eastern Cape, which has tall, unbranched or sparingly branched flowering spikes. *C. aurea*, a smaller (up to 1 m), shade-loving plant, has drooping golden orange flowers in unbranched or weakly branched spikes; cultivated in gardens worldwide, with a number of cultivars (garden montbretias).

Braam van Wyk

Gladiolus alatus

Iridaceae   Spring

Kalkoentjie

Kalkoentjie

Erect perennial, up to 200 mm high, with a corm; occurring singly or as small groups in fynbos and renosterveld of the winter-rainfall area, favouring stony sandstone or granitic soils. Leaves sword-shaped, strongly ribbed. Flowers in racemes, all turned in the same direction, orange, with the three lower petals yellow to greenish and tipped with orange, sweetly scented; upper petal more or less erect. Apparently pollinated by the bee *Anthophora diversipes*. The common name *kalkoentjie* (= little turkey) alludes to the flowers, which resemble the wattles of a turkey (a *kalkoen* in Afrikaans). *G. speciosus* is very similar, but the upper petal is hooded. Also resembles *G. equitans* from Namaqualand, a species which has rather broad (15–45 mm), not prominently ridged, spine-tipped leaves.

John Manning

Gladiolus dalenii

Iridaceae   Spring–Summer

Wild gladiolus

Wildeswaardlelie

An erect perennial, up to 1.5 m high, sprouting annually from a corm; occurring in grassland and bushveld, often in groups among rocks or in bush clumps. Leaves arranged in a fan, erect, 10–30 mm wide, hairless, with prominent ribs. Flowers in erect spikes, large (60–80 mm long), orange to red, with a yellow mark on each of the three lower petals. The most widespread and common member of the more than 250 species of *Gladiolus*. Introduced during the late 1820s from KwaZulu-Natal to European gardens by the Dutch botanist, Cornelius Dalen. One of the parent species used in the breeding of the large-flowered *Gladiolus* cultivars, which is of considerable importance in the cut-flower trade today. Widely used medicinally, although the corms contain toxic compounds, notably saponins.

Braam van Wyk

Watsonia pillansii

Iridaceae   Summer

Large orange watsonia

Grootoranjepypie

Perennial plant, up to 1.2 m high, with a corm; occurring in grassland and fynbos, often in rocky places. Leaves 4–6, strap-shaped, 12–18 mm wide. Flowers usually 25–35 in an erect spike, arranged in two rows and pointing in opposite directions, bright orange to orange-red; perianth with 3 whitish ridges between the lower parts of the filaments. *Watsonia* is a horticulturally important genus of more than 50 species, all confined to southern Africa. There are also species with attractive pink, red, purple, mauve or white flowers. When planting watsonias it is important to note whether the species are from the winter- or summer-rainfall area. Similar to *W. schlechteri*, a montane species with narrower (6–15 mm) leaves from the southwestern parts of the Western Cape.

Leonotis leonurus

Lamiaceae   Summer–Autumn

Wild dagga

Wildedagga

Robust perennial shrub, up to 2 m high, with erect stems from a thick, woody base; occurring along forest margins and in grassland, often in rocky places and on stream banks. Leaves opposite; margin toothed. Flowers in successive, compact whorls, tubular, 2-lipped, densely covered with orange hairs. Parts of the plant, in particular the old seed-containing inflorescences, were once smoked for their narcotic properties. The common names are misleading as it is not at all related to the dagga or marijuana (*Cannabis sativa*) plant. Widely used in traditional medicine to treat a variety of ailments. The generic name, which means 'lion's ears' (from the Greek *leon* = lion + *otis* = ear), refers to the hairy upper lip of the flowers. Flowers pollinated mainly by sunbirds. Popular as a garden ornamental.

Braam van Wyk

65

Leonotis nepetifolia

Lamiaceae Summer–Autumn

Annual wild dagga

Eenjarige wildedagga

Slender, erect, annual or short-lived perennial, up to 3 m tall, slightly branched at the upper nodes only; occurring in bushveld, usually in disturbed sites such as fallow fields and along roadsides. Leaves opposite, broadly ovate with a distinct stalk, 50–200 × 40–150 mm. Flowers in dense spherical clusters grouped at intervals up the stem, tubular, 2-lipped, densely covered with rather dull, pale orange hairs; calyx ± 2-lipped, lobes spine-tipped. A weedy indigenous species, widely distributed northwards in Africa as well as in other tropical parts of the world. Extensively used all over its range in traditional medicine for many different ailments. About eight species of *Leonotis* occur in South Africa, the flowers of which contain abundant nectar and are pollinated by sunbirds.

Braam van Wyk

Salvia africana-lutea (= *S. aurea*)

Lamiaceae Winter–Spring

Golden sage

Bruinsalie

A much-branched, greyish, perennial shrub, up to 2 m high; occurring in fynbos and scrub, often on coastal dunes. Stems densely leafy, with minute orange-red dots. Leaves stalked, thick-textured, densely covered with grey hairs. Flowers in clusters, each comprising several 2-flowered whorls; corolla golden brown, reddish brown or rarely purplish brown, upper lip ± 12 mm long; calyx persistent after flowering, saucer-like, purplish-tinged; bracts broadly ovate or obovate, persistent. The aromatic leaves are used in cooking to flavour food, especially fish, and in traditional medicine to treat colds and coughs. Sometimes confused with brown-flowered forms of *S. lanceolata*, a species with branched inflorescences, deciduous bracts and flowers with the upper lip ± 17 mm long.

Braam van Wyk

Aloe ferox

| Liliaceae | Winter | Bitter aloe
Bitteraalwyn |

Ben-Erik van Wyk

Single-stemmed, unbranched leaf succulent; stem densely covered with old dry leaves; occurring in valley bushveld (thicket), karroid vegetation, coastal bush and grassland, usually on rocky hillsides. Leaves with or without spines on both surfaces; margin with brownish red teeth. Inflorescence branched; flower spikes erect; flowers golden orange to scarlet, rarely white, with tips of inner perianth lobes usually brown or black. Yellowish sap from the leaves is the source of 'Cape aloes', an intensely bitter drug widely used in pharmaceutical preparations, especially for its purgative properties. The jelly-like leaf pulp is used in cosmetic preparations and to prepare a pleasant-tasting health drink. *A. candelabrum*, found in KwaZulu-Natal, tends to have white-tipped perianth lobes.

Aloe marlothii

| Liliaceae | Winter | Mountain aloe
Bergaalwyn |

Norbert Hahn

Single-stemmed, unbranched leaf succulent; stem densely covered with old dry leaves; occurring in bushveld, usually on rocky hillsides. Leaves usually with many spines on both surfaces; margin with reddish brown teeth. Inflorescence branched; flower spikes carried ± horizontally, with the flowers pointing in the same direction (upwards); flowers purplish in bud, opening yellow, orange or bright red, with purple stamens; inner perianth segments tipped dull purple. Ash from the dried leaves is mixed with tobacco snuff. The leaves and sap are used medicinally. *A. spectabilis*, from central KwaZulu-Natal, has spikes that are erect or suberect with the flowers evenly distributed around the axis, with the tips of the inner perianth segments being a glossy black.

Kniphofia linearifolia

Liliaceae   Summer–Autumn

Common marsh poker

Gewone moerasvuurpyl

Robust rhizomatous perennial, up to 1.8 m high; occurring in grassland, usually as dense stands in marshy places. Leaves long and narrow, at first erect, usually bending back under their weight towards maturity, strongly keeled, yellow-green to dull green. Flowers borne well above the reflexed leaves, in dense, ± elongated terminal spikes, drooping, orange-red, pinkish red or dull red in bud, greenish yellow to yellow when open; bracts oblong to blunt or rounded. Most widespread red-hot poker in the region. Very similar to *K. praecox*, a species extensively grown in gardens, which is characterised by sharply pointed, lanceolate bracts. Closely related to *K. rooperi* and *K. uvaria*, both which have roundish flowering spikes. Flowers visited by sunbirds, bees and butterflies.

Braam van Wyk

Papaver aculeatum

Papaveraceae   Summer

Wild poppy

Wildepapawer

Prickly annual herb, up to 1.5 m high, most parts covered with long, stiff, yellowish hairs and spines, and containing milky latex. Occurring in grassland and karroid shrubland, often in disturbed places. Leaves arranged in a basal rosette, or spaced along a sturdy, erect, flowering stem; margin shallowly to deeply pinnately lobed. Flowers borne on long stalks, drooping in bud; petals crinkly, orange to salmon pink. A biogeographical enigma in being the only member of *Papaver* indigenous to the southern hemisphere. It is also peculiar in that plants may suddenly appear at a spot in a particular season, only to vanish without a trace in subsequent years. A very variable species in growth form and floral colour; more than one taxon may be involved. Naturalised in Australia.

Braam van Wyk

Strelitzia reginae

Strelitziaceae   All year   Crane flower / Kraanvoëlblom

A robust, stemless perennial, up to 1.5 m high; occurring in coastal grassland, often in rocky places. Leaves distinctly stalked; blade up to 500 x 100 mm. Flowers ± 6 in a spathe, opening one at a time; the outer three tepals are bright orange and serve for display, the inner three are blue, two being large, forming an arrow-like structure concealing the stamens and style, while the third one is much smaller concealing the nectary. Flower pollination by perching weaver birds and, to a lesser extent, sunbirds. The blue arrow-like structure has two lobes at the base on which birds occasionally stand to feed on the nectar or orange tepals. The weight of the bird pushes the lobes apart, exposing the anthers, which dust the underside of the bird with sticky pollen. A popular garden plant and cutflower worldwide.

Braam van Wyk

Tricliceras longipedunculatum

Turneraceae   Spring–Summer   Roadside pimpernel / Rooihaarbossie

A herb up to 450 mm high, sprouting annually from a perennial taproot; occurring in bushveld, often along roadsides or in fallow lands. Stems with long, reddish purple hairs. Leaves stalkless, linear to oblong, with a few scattered, long, reddish hairs on the midrib below; margin smooth. Flowers in racemes of 7–15 flowers; petals bright orange above, yellowish below. Each flower lasts only one day, but the flowering period extends over a long period. A rich source of toxic chemicals known as pentacyclic cyanogenic glycosides, the plants serve as food for the larvae of several butterflies of the genus *Acraea*. These compounds are accumulated by the butterfly larvae and eventually end up in the mature butterflies, thus rendering both stages toxic or distasteful to predators such as birds.

Darrel Plowes

Anisotes rogersii

Acanthaceae   Summer–Autumn

Limpopo anisotes

Limpopo-anisotes

A deciduous perennial shrublet, up to 1.5 m high; occurring in hot, arid, frost-free areas, often in mopane or *Acacia* woodland. Young branches round or angled, but not grooved, greyish. Leaves opposite or clustered on reduced shoots, narrowly elliptic or ovate, 30–80 × 15–35 mm; stalk up to 2 mm long. Flowers axillary, produced in clusters; corolla tubular, 2-lipped, 38–60 mm long, red to orange; upper lip slightly arched, with tip 2-fid. Capsules obovoid, flattened, 25–30 mm long, 8 mm wide. The species is locally abundant in the Limpopo River Valley. Following good rains, mass flowering of plants can turn the veld into a blaze of colour. Pollinated by sunbirds. *A. formosissimus*, from further north in southern Africa, has the new branches 4-angled, grooved and greenish, with flowers in spikes.

Piet van Wyk–Agfa

Crossandra greenstockii

Acanthaceae   Spring–Summer

Bushveld crossandra

Bosveld-crossandra

An erect perennial herb, up to 300 mm high, sprouting annually from a woody rootstock; occurring in bushveld. Leaves ± oval, mostly in a basal rosette, hairy, narrowing to a stalk-like base. Flowers in dense spikes, with the inflorescence stalk usually unbranched; corolla with a long, very narrow tube and a flaring, 5-lobed lip, ± 20 mm wide, bright orange-red; bracts large (25 × 18 mm), overlapping, green, with long-stalked glandular hairs, margin with a few short teeth or smooth. When the dry capsules are wetted by rain, they split explosively, ejecting the seed some distance from the plant. Upon wetting, flat hairs on the seed uncurl and become sticky, causing them to adhere to wet soil. Similar to *C. zuluensis,* which has almost hairless bracts and larger flowers (± 30 mm wide).

Braam van Wyk & Sasa Malan

Ammocharis coranica

Amaryllidaceae Spring Sore-eye flower / Seeroogblom

A deciduous perennial with a large bulb; occurring in grassland, bushveld and karroid vegetation, usually in groups. Leaves radiating on or near the ground, strap-shaped, older ones blunt-tipped (died back). Flowers in a globose head borne on a flattened stalk, sweetly scented; perianth silvery pink, segments recurved; anthers white. Plants grow very old; larger ones may be well over 100 years. Bulb contains several poisonous alkaloids. Used for medicinal and magical purposes; fresh bulb scales are lightly fried and applied as a dressing to open wounds and boils. A paste prepared from the cooked bulb is used to repair cracks in clay pots. Caterpillars of the lily leaf miner (*Brithys crini pancratii*) often bore inside the leaf tissue, but they do not usually attack the bulb.

Boophane disticha

Amaryllidaceae Spring Poison bulb / Kopseerblom

A deciduous perennial; bulb partly exposed above the ground; occurring mainly in grassland and bushveld. Leaves erect, arranged in a conspicuous fan, greyish green, usually produced after flowering. Flowers in a globose head, deep pink, sweetly scented; flower stalks lengthen considerably during the fruiting stage to form a large ball. Larger bulbs may be several centuries old. Dry fruiting heads roll about in the wind, dispersing the seeds in the manner of a tumble weed. Exposure to flowers may result in headaches and sore eyes (apparently caused by the penetrating scent). Bulb poisonous due to the presence of numerous alkaloids, although widely used in traditional medicine; bulb scales are a popular dressing for wounds, sometimes after being soaked in olive or linseed-oil.

Braam van Wyk & Sasa Malan

71

Brunsvigia radulosa

Amaryllidaceae — Summer

Pink candelabra flower — Pienkkandelaarblom

Deciduous perennial with a large bulb; occurring in grassland, karroid vegetation and bushveld. Leaves ± 4, pressed close to the ground, appearing with or after flowering. Flowers in an umbel at the end of a sturdy, erect stalk, bright pink; flower stalks lengthen considerably during fruiting. Fruiting heads roll about in the wind, scattering the seed as they rotate. Bulb used medicinally. Genus with about 20 species, mainly southern African. Flowers pinkish red or crimson in *B. grandiflora* and *B. natalensis*. Leaves 10–15 and erect in the former, 2–5 and semi-erect in the latter. Both occur in the eastern and northeastern parts of the region and are summer-growing. *B. orientalis*, a red-flowered, winter-growing species from the Western Cape, usually has the flower stalks tinged with red.

Darrel Plowes

Crinum bulbispermum

Amaryllidaceae — Spring

Vaal River Lily — Hoëveldse vleilelie

Perennial, with a large bulb; occurring in grassland, usually along rivers and in marshy places. Leaves arching, strap-shaped, folded upward along the midrib; margin often wavy. Flowers clustered at the end of a tall, sturdy, erect, inflorescence stalk, ± drooping when open; perianth white or pale to dark pink, with a dark pink keel; anthers greyish or pale brown. Fruits large with many green and roundish, fleshy seeds, tipped by a scar. Attractive garden plant. The fleshy seeds germinate readily without water, even while still in the fruit. Bulb highly poisonous due to the presence of various alkaloids; extensively used in traditional medicine, usually in small amounts and mixed with other ingredients. Similar to *C. macowanii,* which tends to have black anthers.

Braam van Wyk & Sasa Malan

Crinum delagoense

Candy-striped crinum

Amaryllidaceae   Spring   Gestreepte vleilelie

Trevor Coleman

Perennial with a large bulb; occurring in coastal grassland and in low-altitude bushveld, usually on sandy soils. Leaves sprawling on the ground, strap-shaped, ± flat; margin with fine hairs. Flowers clustered at the end of a short, sturdy, arching, inflorescence stalk, ± drooping when open; perianth white to pink, with a dark pink keel; anthers greyish or pale brown. Fruits large, pinkish red, with many roundish, fleshy seeds, tipped by a scar. Conspicuous in coastal grassland of Maputaland. Attractive garden plant; flowers having a distinct striped appearance. Bulb used in traditional remedies to treat people and cattle. Similar in habit to *C. graminicola*, a species of Highveld grassland, which has ± uniformly deep pink flowers and fruit tipped by an elongated protuberance (beak).

Nerine sarniensis

Red nerine

Amaryllidaceae   Summer–Autumn   Rooinerina

Braam van Wyk

Bulbous perennial; occurring in fynbos. Leaves ± 6, strap-shaped, produced after or with the flowers. Flowers in an umbel at the end of an erect inflorescence stalk, bright scarlet. Pollinated by the satyrid butterfly *Aeropetes tulbaghia* (Table Mountain beauty). Also known as the Guernsey lily, it is cultivated in gardens worldwide and has been used in the breeding of many nerine cultivars. Endemic to the Western Cape, its establishment on Guernsey was due to a Dutch ship, homeward bound via the Cape from the Far East, that was wrecked on the Channel Islands in 1659. It carried a consignment of Cape bulbs, some of which washed out and established on the shores of Guernsey and other islands. The ± 30 species of *Nerine* are, however, all native to southern Africa.

73

Scadoxus puniceus

Amaryllidaceae

Spring

Red paintbrush

Rooikwas

Braam van Wyk

Deciduous perennial with a bulbous rhizome; occurring in grassland, bushveld and along forest margins, usually in rocky or shady places. Leaves erect, clasping at the base to form a short false stem; margin wavy; midrib distinct; leaf stalk purple-spotted. Flowers in a dense cluster ('brush') surrounded by large bracts; perianth indistinct; filaments conspicuous, scarlet; anthers yellow. Fruit a berry, red. Bulbs poisonous, used in traditional medicine. *S. membranaceous*, from forest along the east coast, also has a congested inflorescence enclosed by large bracts, but it lacks a false stem. *S. multiflorus* has flowers with longer stalks and well-developed, spreading tepals, resulting in more rounded inflorescences; an attractive container plant for shady places.

Pachypodium succulentum

Apocynaceae

Spring

Mountain kambroo

Bergkambroo

Gerald Cubitt

Spiny, succulent perennial shrublet, up to 600 mm high, with milky latex and a large, half-submerged tuber; occurring in arid, karroid vegetation. Leaves stalkless, alternate or in tufts, linear to linear-lanceolate, green and hairy above, with a white wool below; stipules spiny, borne on a cushion around base of leaf. Flowers in terminal clusters, crimson or shades of pink, rarely white, usually with a darker stripe; corolla lobes tapering to a point, 8–18 mm long. Fruit elongated, paired, appearing horn-like. The turnip-shaped tuber is edible. It is either consumed fresh, or used to brew an alcoholic beer or to prepare a yeast for baking bread. A pleasantly flavoured jam is cooked from young tubers. *P. bispinosum* from the Eastern Cape has shorter (5–7 mm long) and more rounded corolla lobes.

Hoodia gordonii

Asclepiadaceae   Summer

Baboon ghaap
Bobbejaanghaap

Erect, leafless, suc-
culent perennial up
to 750 mm high,
with a watery latex;
occurring in semidesert vegetation, often in extensive colonies.
Stems thick, cylindrical, with
11–17 longitudinal ridges bearing
regularly spaced tubercles tipped
by greyish or brownish spines.
Flowers ± circular, flat and saucer-
shaped, produced in profusion
near tip of stems, large (50–100
mm in diameter), flesh-coloured to
purple-red with darker veins, unpleasantly scented; pollinated by
flies. Used in traditional medicine.
The specific name honours the
pioneering Dutch explorer and
naturalist Colonel R.J. Gordon
(1743–1795), who first collected the plant, supposedly in the vicinity
of Upington, between 1778 and 1780. He also painted the species;
the original painting is now in the Rijksmuseum, in Amsterdam.

Robert Archer

Microloma sagittatum

Asclepiadaceae   Winter–Spring

Pink kannetjies
Pienkkannetjies

Twining perennial
herb with slender
stems and milky
latex; occurring in
semidesert vegetation, usually in
rocky places. Leaves opposite, narrow, arrow-shaped, up to 25 mm
long; margin recurved. Flowers in
loose clusters, ± 7 mm long, erect;
corolla tubular, 5-angled, pink, the
petals hardly spreading (flowers
appear closed). Pollinated by sunbirds, which carry the sticky
pollinia on the tongue from one
flower to another. The flowers
contain abundant sweet nectar.
This is sucked from the flowers by
children, hence the Afrikaans common name (*kannetjies* = little
cans). Plants are very palatable to
sheep and goats. *M. namaquense* has red flowers with the tips of the
petals rounded and overlapping in a spiral rosette. *M. calycinum* has
large, spreading, reddish pink, petal-like sepals.

Neil Crouch

75

*Cosmos bipinnatus (= *Bidens formosa*)   Cosmos

Asteraceae   Autumn   Kosmos

Bushy annual herb, up to 2 m high; occurring mainly in grassland, usually in dense stands along roadsides, in cultivated lands and in other disturbed places. Leaves opposite, stalked and stem-clasping; blade deeply and finely divided. Flower heads radiate (see page 140); ray florets red, pink or white; disc florets yellow. A native of the southern USA and Mexico. Introduced to South Africa with animal fodder in late 1890s. First recorded as a naturalised weed near Pretoria in 1904, only reaching Kwa-Zulu-Natal in 1945. Now well established throughout the cool and wet parts of the Highveld, where mass blooming of plants creates spectacular flower displays in autumn. The proportion of white, pink and red flowers varies from place to place. Generic name from the Greek *kosmos* = beautiful.

Braam van Wyk

Gerbera jamesonii   Barberton daisy

Asteraceae   Spring–Summer   Barbertonse madeliefie

Stemless herb with a perennial root-stock; occurring in bushveld, often in semishade. Leaves with margin unevenly and deeply lobed and toothed. Flower heads radiate (see page 140), ± 80 mm in diameter; ray florets usually deep orange-red to red; disc florets yellow to orange. Probably the best-known contribution to horticulture to come from the South African bushveld; gerbera cultivars, in a rich variety of colours, are popular garden plants and cut flowers throughout the world. Most were derived from hybrids made by a British nurseryman, Richard Irwin Lynch, in about 1890. About 15 species of *Gerbera* occur in the region. *G. aurantiaca* has bright orange-red ray florets, disc florets with black anthers and leaves that are ± smooth. It occurs in grassland, mainly in KwaZulu-Natal.

Braam van Wyk

Helichrysum adenocarpum

Asteraceae   Summer

Pink everlasting

Pienksewejaartjie

Herb up to 450 mm high with a perennial rootstock; occurring in grassland, often in large colonies on moist slopes. Leaves in one–several rosettes, basal ones ± flat on the ground, 20–40 × 15–25 mm, grey, woolly, ± prostrate. Flowering stems emerging from the side of rosettes, erect, simple or branching above, covered by smaller, narrow, woolly leaves; flower heads (see page 140) 15–20 mm long, 25–35 mm in diameter; bracts glossy, white, or white tipped pink, crimson or scarlet; centre yellow, often tipped red. Heads open fully only in bright sunlight, close towards evening. Dried flower heads retain their colour; used in dried-flower arrangements. In *H. monticola* the flowering stems emerge from the centre of the leaf rosettes; found mainly in the Drakensberg Escarpment and foothills.

Lal Greene

Helichrysum ecklonis

Asteraceae   Spring–Summer

Giant pink everlasting

Reusepienksewejaartjie

Herb up to 500 mm high, with a perennial rootstock; occurring in grassland, usually as isolated tufts. Leaves in one–several rosettes, basal ones ± flat on the ground, up to 200 × 20 mm, loosely covered in grey, woolly hairs, especially on the lower surface. Flowering stems emerging from the centre of rosettes, erect, unbranched, covered by smaller, narrow, woolly leaves; flower heads 25–30 mm long, ± 55 mm in diameter; bracts glossy, white to deep rose pink; centre yellow. Flower heads (see page 140) used in dried-flower arrangements. Named after the plant collector, Christian Ecklon (1795–1868). *H. vernum*, from the high Drakensberg between KwaZulu-Natal and Lesotho, has similar flower heads, but this species forms dense mats.

Braam van Wyk

Phaenocoma prolifera

Asteraceae   Summer

Pink Cape everlasting

Rooisewejaartjie

Rigid, evergreen, much-branched perennial shrublet, up to 600 mm high; occurring in fynbos on sandy, acidic soils, often on rocky coastal mountain slopes and along roadsides. Stems covered with dense, short wool. Leaves very small and scale-like, crowded on short side branches, greyish green. Flower heads (see page 140) large and showy; bracts numerous, glossy, deep pink, fading pale pink to whitish; centre white. Plants are aromatic and harsh, hence they are not browsed by animals. Flower heads used in dried-flower arrangements. Old flower heads may remain on the plant for many months. The only member of the genus. *Edmondia pinifolia*, a pink everlasting from the same general area, has ± unbranched stems and flower heads with a yellow centre.

John Manning

Senecio elegans

Asteraceae   Spring

Purple senecio

Strandblommetjie

Robust, bushy annual, up to 600 mm high; occurring in strandveld and fynbos, often on coastal sand dunes. Stems with rough hairs. Leaves deeply once or twice divided and ± curly, with rough hairs, often ± sticky; margins rolled under. Flower heads (see page 140) in branched, flat-topped inflorescences, ± 25 mm in diameter; ray florets 12–14, magenta; disc florets yellow; base of head globose, involucral bracts in a single row, hairless, black-tipped. Plants near the seashore tend to have more fleshy leaves. An attractive annual for the garden; sow seed in March. Unpalatable to livestock. *S. arenarius*, also with bicoloured heads, is a more slender plant with the base of the flower head cylindrical, hairy, with 1–3 small involucral bracts. It is part of the floral display in Namaqualand.

Braam van Wyk

Senecio speciosus

Asteraceae — Spring

Beautiful senecio
Pienk-senecio

Martin von Fintel

Perennial herb with a stout, woody root-stock; occurring in grassland and fyn-bos, usually in moist places. Leaves mainly in a basal rosette, spatulate or elliptic, ± 100–200 × 20–40 mm, usually with sticky (glandular) hairs; base tapering, broad, flat and stalk-like, stem-clasping; margin pinnately lobed, margin of lobes often toothed. Several flowering stems form from the same crown, often slightly reclining at the base, then erect, branched above; flower heads (see page 140) ± 12–15 mm in diameter; ray florets 18–14, they and the disc florets are pink to purple. Used in traditional medicine for various ailments. Attractive plant for frost-free gardens. *S. macrocephalus*, also with similar-coloured disc and ray florets, has ± stalkless leaves with the margin often ± smooth or very shallowly toothed.

*Zinnia peruviana

Asteraceae — Summer–Autumn

Redstar zinnia
Wildejakobregop

Braam van Wyk

Slender, erect annual herb, up to 500 mm high; occurring in grassland and bush-veld, often in disturbed or shady places. Leaves stalkless, opposite, widely spaced, covered with rough hairs. Flowers heads (see page 140) solitary, at the ends of stalks, which gradually thicken towards the head; ray florets red or pale orange, persistent, drying to purplish brown; centre conical, brownish or yellow. A native of South America, now naturalised in many parts of the world. Not a serious weed in agricultural land. The genus contains ± 11 species, some of which were already grown by the Aztecs. Cultivars of the Mexican *Z. violacea* are popular garden ornamentals (zinnias); they come in all colours, except blue. The generic name honours Johann Gottfried Zinn (1727–1759), a German professor of Botany at Gottingen.

Impatiens sylvicola

Balsaminaceae   Summer

Forest impatiens
Woud-impatiens

Soft, erect herbace-ous annual or peren-nial, up to 400 mm high; occurring in damp, shady places in forest, often in forest clearings or along forest paths and roads. Leaves broadly ovate to ± elliptic; margin finely and bluntly toothed; stalk up to 35 mm long. Flowers irregu-lar, pink or purplish pink with a deep mauve or reddish blotch towards the base of the two upper side petals; one of the sepals spur-red. Plants often occur in dense stands. The fleshy fruits open ex-plosively to scatter the seed; this response can be triggered by gently squeezing the tip of a ripe capsule. *I. hochstetteri* is another common forest species in the region. It has a paler pink flower with the two lower (front) petals narrower and the two upper side ones larger. Several species grown as garden and house plants.

Braam van Wyk

*Canna indica

Cannaceae   Summer–Autumn

Wild canna
Wildekanna

Perennial herb, up to 1.5 m high, with annual stems from a swollen tuberous rhizome: occurring in moist grass-land and along forest margins. Leaves large, broad, pinnately veined with a distinct midrib; stalk present, sheathing the stem. Flowers in racemes at the ends of erect stems; sepals and petals 3 each, green; showy part of flowers formed by sterile, red, petal-like stamens, the largest of these being orange-red, reflexed and rolled back on itself. Fruit a warty capsule. Black seeds used as beads. The genus is native to Central America and the West Indies. Several cultivars are grown as greenhouse and garden ornamentals; many developed from *C. indica*. *C. edulis* is of considerable economic importance as the source of a starch known as purple or Queensland arrowroot.

Braam van Wyk

Ipomoea crassipes

Convolvulaceae Spring–Summer

Leafy-flowered ipomoea

Pienkpatat

Herb with trailing or ± erect annual stems from a perennial tuberous rootstock; occurring mainly in grassland. Leaves very variable, usually ovate to lanceolate, 15–80 × 8–30 mm, hairy, often with a purplish margin; stalk up to 10 mm long. Flowers solitary; calyx surrounded by leaf-like bracts; corolla funnel-shaped, 35–60 mm in diameter, magenta or pale mauve, rarely white with a dark purple centre. Fruit a dehiscent capsule, ± 10 mm in diameter. Very variable in leaf shape and habit, but the presence of leaf-like bracts below the calyx is diagnostic. Tuber used medicinally against dysentery, sores and hiccups; it is also said to be edible. About 50 species of *Ipomoea* are native to the region. *I. batatas*, originally from Central America, is the cultivated sweet potato.

Ipomoea ommaneyi

Convolvulaceae Summer

Silver-leafed ipomoea

Beespatat

Prostrate perennial herb; tuber is very large (at least 1 × 0.3 m), with robust (up to 10 mm in diameter), annual, trailing stems; occurring in grassland and bushveld. Leaves all pointing upwards, ovate-lanceolate or oblong-lanceolate, very large (up to 300 × 120 mm), both surfaces sparsely covered with silvery white hairs; margin wavy with a dense fringe of yellowish hairs. Flowers clustered together in dense heads on erect stalks; corolla funnel-shaped, rose-magenta, with distinct midpetaline areas that are white and densely silky outside. Most readily noticed by its robust trailing stems and large, silvery leaves. Formerly crushed dried roots were mixed with curdled milk or with water and used as a famine food. Grazed by livestock. Larger tubers may be centuries old.

81

Ipomoea pes-caprae
Convolvulaceae   Summer–Autumn   Dune morning glory   Duinpatat

Perennial herb, with long-trailing stems rooting at the nodes, sprouting from a tuberous rootstock; milky latex present; occurring on sandy beaches. Leaves rounded and ± 2-lobed, thick and leathery, up to 100 mm in diameter, hairless; stalk usually up to 120 mm long. Flowers solitary or in clusters on a stout, erect stalk; corolla funnel-shaped, ± 60 mm in diameter, pink, magenta or purple, darker inside at the base. Common pioneer (sand-binder) on tropical beaches; usually growing just above the high-water mark. Midrib below with two glands (extrafloral nectaries) at the leaf base; these attract ants for protection. Tuber, leaves and seed used medicinally; leaves show anti-inflammatory activity. Specific name means 'like a goat's foot', and refers to the shape of the leaves.

Tony Abbott

Turbina oblongata (= *Ipomoea oblongata*)
Convolvulaceae   Summer   Grassland turbina   Grasveld-valspatat

Perennial herb, with annual prostrate stems from a large tuber; occurring in grassland and bushveld. Leaves with short stalks, ± erect, usually ovate or elliptic, 20–100 × 15–50 mm, upper surface sparsely and lower surface sparsely or densely covered with yellowish hairs; margin ± wavy, with a fringe of hairs. Flowers usually solitary, on erect stalks; outer sepals ± densely covered with stiff, yellowish hairs; corolla funnel-shaped, ± 60 mm in diameter, magenta. In large plants the tubers may be well over a century old; seeds are rarely produced. Tuber and leaves used in traditional medicine. *Turbina* and *Ipomoea* are very similar in vegetative and floral characters. They differ primarily in their capsular fruit; those of the former being indehiscent, the latter dehiscent by 4, rarely 6 valves.

Braam van Wyk & Sasa Malan

Turbina oenotheroides (= *Ipomoea oenotheroides*) Christmas flower
Convolvulaceae Summer Krismisblom

Erect much-branched shrublet, up to 1 m high, sprouting from perennial tuberous roots; occurring in grassland and karroid vegetation, often along roadsides. Leaves linear to lanceolate, usually 3–6 × 2–8 mm; stalk usually up to 6 mm long. Flowers solitary on slender stalks in leaf axils; corolla funnel-shaped, 35–70 mm in diameter, bright magenta or magenta-pink, midpetaline areas usually densely covered with short, appressed, silvery hairs. Plants tend to grow in large colonies. They flower around Christmas, hence the common name. Flowers open after sunrise, fade by midday. They are fed on by yellow-and-black CMR beetles (*Mylabris oculata*), which consume the corolla as soon as it opens in the morning. The tuber is said to be inedible.

Braam van Wyk

Cotyledon orbiculata Pig's ears
Crassulaceae Winter–Spring Plakkie

Robust perennial succulent, with erect or reclining stems with the tips growing upward; occurring in karroid vegetation, thicket, bushveld and rocky places in grassland. Leaves very variable in shape, usually ± flattened, greyish green, with a white powdery bloom; margin reddish. Flowers in compact clusters at the end of a sturdy, erect stalk, pendulous; corolla ± cylindrical with recurved lobes, orange or pinkish red. Pollinated mainly by honeybees. The leaves, applied as a dressing, are a popular and effective traditional remedy to treat corns and warts. Plants are toxic because of the presence of several cardiac glycosides of the bufadienolide type; cause *krimpsiekte* in domestic animals, especially sheep and goats. Poisoning may be acute or chronic, the latter due to the cumulative effect of the toxin.

Braam van Wyk & Sasa Malan

83

Crassula perfoliata (= *C. falcata*)

Crassulaceae   Autumn–Spring

Flat-leaved crassula

Platblaarplakkie

An evergreen, erect, little-branched succulent up to 1.5 m high; occurring in thicket or rocky places in grassland. Stems are covered with coarse, ± rounded papillae. Leaves opposite or ± in a fan, very variable, ± finger-like, flat or laterally compressed, 40–120 x 12–35 mm, green to grey, densely covered with coarse, rounded, erect papillae. Flowers numerous, congested in a rounded, flat-topped inflorescence at the end of an erect stalk, the latter with reduced leaves; corolla tubular, fused basally for 1–1.5 mm, white, pink to scarlet, lobes 3–6 mm long; stamens with black anthers. This is a variable species with a number of distinct forms; var. *minor*, with laterally flattened leaves, is illustrated here. A handsome plant that does well in dry rockeries.

Braam van Wyk

Erica cerinthoides

Ericaceae   All year

Fire heath

Rooihaartjie

Erect shrublet, up to 500 mm high, sprouting from a perennial rootstock; occurring in fynbos and grassland, often in rocky places. Leaves in clusters, needle-like, glandular. Flowers in clusters at ends of branches; corolla tubular, usually 25–35 mm long (± 12 mm in var. *barbertona*), dark pinkish red or rarely white tipped red, with spreading hairs; anthers without appendages. Most widespread erica in the region, and one of a mere handful that occurs in the summer-rainfall area. Flowering is stimulated by fire. *Erica* derives from the Greek *ereike*, a name used for a heath by Pliny and Theophrastus. More than 760 of some 860 *Erica* species found worldwide occur in the region. Of these, 730 occur in the Cape Floristic Region, making it the most species-rich genus in the country.

Braam van Wyk

Erica mammosa

Ericaceae Summer–Autumn

Nipple erica

Rooiklossieheide

Slender, erect shrublet up to 1.8 m high; occurring in fynbos, often in sandy seepage areas. Leaves needle-like, overlapping. Flowers in loose spikes near ends of branches, drooping; corolla tubular, slightly puffed, 24–26 mm long, usually bright red, but also white, orange, pink, purple or green, with four indents at the base of the tube; anthers with tail-like appendages. A hardy species occasionally grown in gardens, even in areas with winter frost. Like most ericas it requires a sunny position and well-drained, acidic, sandy soil, that is rich in humus. All ericas have roots with special fungal associates (mycorrhizas). The specific name is from the Latin *mammosus* = with breasts; presumably referring to the shape of the flowers, which resemble a cow's teats.

John Manning

Erica plukenetii

Ericaceae All year

Hangertjie

Hangertjie

Erect shrublet, with ± feathery foliage, up to 1 m high; hairless; occurring in fynbos, on mountain slopes and flats. Leaves arranged in successive whorls on the branches, needle-like, usually 12–16 mm long. Flowers in densely packed spikes, usually some distance below the tips of shoots, drooping; corolla tubular and inflated, 13–18 mm long, pink, reddish purple, red-orange or sometimes white with green lobes; anthers positioned at tip of filaments, long (up to 12 mm) and narrow, brownish, projecting conspicuously far beyond the corolla tube, without tail-like appendages. Flowers pollinated by sunbirds. Similar to *E. coccinea*, which has shorter leaves (4–8 mm) arranged in tufts, and a whorl of sepal-like bracts below and partly overlapping with the calyx.

John Manning

85

Erica pulchella

Ericaceae   Spring–Autumn

Pink-spike erica

Pienkaarheide

Floriferous, bushy perennial herb with many erect stems, up to 600 mm high; occurring in fynbos, often in dense stands on dry sandy flats and lower mountain slopes. Leaves needle-like, pointing towards tips of stems. Flowers in leaf axils towards ends of branches, often in a spike-like formation; corolla bell-shaped, 3–4 mm long, lobes slightly spreading, pale pink to dark red, occasionally white; anthers do not protrude from the corolla, each one has two, slender, tail-like appendages at the base. Very variable as to flower colour and flowering time. Young plants tend to be more floriferous than the older ones. Very similar to *E. longiaristata* from the Bredasdorp District, a more spreading and lax shrublet with flowers that have a slightly wider mouth.

Colin Paterson-Jones

Erica sparsa (= *E. floribunda*)

Ericaceae   Winter–Spring

Kerker

Kerker

Floriferous, bushy perennial shrublet, up to 1 m high; occurring mainly in fynbos and grassy fynbos, often in dense colonies on hillsides and in clearings. Leaves small and needle-like. Flowers very small, produced in masses along stems, usually completely concealing the leaves; calyx short, pink or, rarely, white; corolla cup-shaped with an open mouth, ± 1 mm long, pale pink or, rarely, white; anthers dark purple, not protruding, without tail-like appendages; style protruding, pink. The common name is said to be onomatopoeic, being a representation of the harsh, grating noise that is produced when one walks through the plants, or when the wheels of a cart ride over them. This plant is very common in the Tsitsikamma area, especially along roadsides.

Gerald Cubitt

Erica versicolor

Ericaceae   Winter–Spring

Tall sticky erica

Groottaaiheide

Sturdy shrub, up to 3 m high, with branches straight or variously curved; occurring in fynbos, usually on lower mountain slopes and along roadsides. Leaves small, needle-like. Flowers clustered at the ends of branches; corolla tubular, 22–28 mm long, usually with a red base and a greenish to white tip, very sticky; stamens included; anthers borne on the side of each filament, without tail-like appendages. The flowers are pollinated by sunbirds. Glossy outer appearance of the corolla is due to a very sticky secretion that probably serves to deter non-pollinating nectar-eating insects. This is supported by the observation that insects are often seen trapped on the corolla, as if caught on flypaper. Sticky corollas are found in several native erica species.

Gerald Cubitt

Indigofera heterophylla

Fabaceae   Spring

Lucerne bush

Boontjiekaroo

Prostrate perennial shrublet, up to 300 mm high, often scrambling over other plants; occurring in fynbos, grassland and karroid vegetation, often in rocky places. Leaves trifoliolate; leaflets ± 10 x 5 mm, dark green; stalk up to 15 mm long. Flowers (see page 140) in short, erect racemes at the ends of stems, bright pink to brick red. Pods cylindrical, ± 20 mm long. A valuable grazing bush that is highly palatable to livestock; one of the first species to disappear from overgrazed veld. Leaves are reminiscent of those of lucerne, hence the English common name. About 200 species of *Indigofera* are native to the region. Those from the Cape Floristic Region tend to have more pinkish flowers, whereas those with reddish flowers tend to predominate in other areas where these plants occur.

John Manning

Indigofera hilaris

Fabaceae   Spring

Grassland indigofera
Grasveld-indigofera

Perennial shrublet with erect, sparsely branched stems from a woody tuber; occurring in grassland. Stems with non-glandular, appressed hairs. Leaves pinnately compound, greyish green; leaflets 5, 2 opposite pairs with a terminal one. Flowers (see page 140) in axillary racemes, which are often shorter than the leaves, pink to reddish pink. Flowers profusely after fire. One of the typical pre-rain flowers in the Grassland Biome. The generic name comes from indigo, the blue dye (Greek: *indicos* = of India, whence the dye originally comes) and *fero*, to produce. The dye is primarily obtained from *I. tinctoria* (Southeast Asia) and *I. dimidiata* (called *I. arrecta* in southern Africa). Branches are subjected to a rather complicated fermentation process. Today, however, the dye is produced synthetically.

Braam van Wyk

Indigofera sanguinea

Fabaceae   Spring–Summer

Blood-red indigofera
Bloedrooi-indigofera

A spreading perennial shrublet with erect shoots, up to 600 mm high, sprouting annually from a tuberous rootstock; occurring in grassland, often in rocky places. Leaves pinnately compound; leaflets ± 7 pairs, ± 10 x 7 mm each. Flowers (see page 140) in dense, erect racemes, bright orange-red. Pods cylindrical, ± 40 x 2 mm, hairy. *Indigofera* flowers have evolved a fascinating explosive pollen-presentation mechanism. In the newly opened flower the stamen tube is held under tension between the keel petals by projections on their upper edges. The pressure exerted by a visiting bee dislodges these projections, releasing the stamen tube and style, which spring up, forcefully striking the underside of the visitor. Once 'exploded', the spent flower hangs limply open.

Braam van Wyk

Pseudarthria hookeri

Fabaceae   Summer–Autumn

Velvet bean
Fluweelboontjie

A robust, sparsely branched, erect perennial, up to 3 m high, sprouting annually from a woody rootstock; occurring on forest margins, associated grassland and in bushveld, often along roadsides. Stems angular, velvety, Leaves trifoliolate; leaflets ± 70 x 40 mm, dark green with rough hairs above, whitish green with dense hairs below. Flowers (see page 140) in large terminal panicles, bright pink. Pods 12–38 x 3–4 mm, velvety. Plants often appear top-heavy and bend down under the weight of the large inflorescences. Curled hairs on the leaves enable them to stick to clothing. The hairy pods adhere to passing objects. Leafy branches are used to catch bedbugs; placed around a sleeping person at night, the bugs are trapped between the dense hairs on the leaves and stems.

Braam van Wyk

Sphenostylis angustifolia

Fabaceae   Spring–Summer

Wild sweetpea
Wilde-ertjie

Perennial shrublet with spreading to erect annual stems from a woody rootstock, up to 400 mm high; occurring in grassland, especially in rocky places. Leaves trifoliolate, with stalk 20–80 mm long; leaflets ± 40 x 5–10 mm. Flowers (see page 140) 1–4 at the end of an erect inflorescence stalk; corolla bright pink with a yellow blotch on the standard petal, rarely white fading to cream, keel twisted. Flowering is stimulated by late winter fires. Deflection of the keel and style to one side is known as enantiostyly or enantiomorphy; flowers may be either left- or right-handed, depending on the plant. The stylar deflection results in pollen deposition on one side of the bee's abdomen, and is a special adaptation to facilitate cross-pollination and outcrossing. Leaf infusions used in traditional medicine.

Braam van Wyk & Sasa Malan

Sutherlandia frutescens

Fabaceae — Spring–Summer

Cancer bush — Kankerbos

Short-lived perennial shrublet, up to 1 m high; occurring in fynbos and karroid vegetation, often along roadsides. Leaves pinnately compound with numerous small leaflets, silvery grey due to a dense cover of silvery hairs. Flowers (see page 140) in clusters, bright red. Pods inflated, papery, reddish-tinged when young. Flowers pollinated by sunbirds; seed dispersed when pods are blown around by wind. A popular traditional remedy (extremely bitter-tasting) for a variety of ailments, including colds, influenza, diabetes, varicose veins, liver problems and cancer. Plants are very palatable to livestock and of high nutritional value; may give milk a bitter taste. The species of *Sutherlandia* (about six) are all very similar-looking and difficult to tell apart. The group contains anticancer compounds.

Jeremy Hollmann

Tephrosia grandiflora

Fabaceae — All year

Large pink tephrosia — Grootpienk-tephrosia

An erect annual or short-lived perennial shrublet, up to 1.5 m high; occurring in bushveld and grassland. Leaflets 3–5 pairs, ± 15 × 6 mm, with fine silvery grey hairs below; stipules narrowly ovate, ± 10–32 mm long, longer than wide. Flowers (see page 140) pea-like, clustered in terminal racemes, are large (± 20 mm long), bright magenta-pink. Pods ± 30 × 8 mm, many-seeded. Attractive garden plant. Root infusions used to treat chest ailments. Like other members of the genus the plant contains tephrosin, rotenone and related compounds that have strong insecticidal and piscicidal properties. Pounded leaves, pods or roots thrown into a pool suffocate fish, thus paralysing them so that they can be easily caught. Fish so poisoned can be eaten without ill effect.

Trevor Coleman

Chironia baccifera

Gentianaceae   Spring

Christmas berry

Aambeibossie

Evergreen, rounded, much-branched perennial shrublet, up to 1 m high; occurring in fynbos, grassland, and especially coastal dune vegetation. Stems angular or narrowly winged. Leaves inconspicuous, stalkless, thin to ± fleshy, 5–20 × 1–3 mm; margin rolled downward. Flowers ± solitary, scattered all over bush, pink; anthers yellow. Fruit berry-like, produced in abundance, bright red, drying black. A popular traditional medicine; extensively used as a blood purifier to treat skin problems, boils and haemorrhoids. Infusions are bitter-tasting and have a strong purgative action; also used as an external application. The plant is said to be potentially toxic and it should only be taken internally when administered by a knowledgeable person. Plants are easily propagated from seed, but they are frost-sensitive.

Chironia palustris

Gentianaceae   Spring–Summer

Marsh chironia

Bitterwortel

Erect, bushy perennial herb, up to 700 mm high; occurring in grassland, often forming dense clumps in marshy places and along stream banks. Leaves initially in a basal rosette, blue-green, ± succulent. Flowers in terminal, well-spaced groups, ± 25 mm in diameter, bright rose-pink; calyx ± as long as corolla tube; anthers slightly twisted; buds with calyx lobes and bracts not tapering into a long slender point. Calyx lobes sometimes ± sticky and function as extrafloral nectaries attracting ants. Root used medicinally to treat colic and diarrhoea; plants may be poisonous. About 15 species of *Chironia* are native to South Africa. *C. purpurascens* (with ± the same range) has deep magenta-pink flowers, calyx lobes longer than the corolla tube and buds with calyx lobes and bracts tapering to a long point.

Pelargonium cucullatum

Geraniaceae   Spring

Hooded-leaf pelargonium

Wildemalva

A sturdy, bushy perennial shrublet, up to 2 m high; occurring in fynbos, usually in dense stands in coastal areas. Woody at the base, young stems ± herbaceous. Leaves ± kidney-shaped, pleated, up to 45–60 mm, sometimes ± cup-shaped (hooded), with long, soft hairs; margin irregularly toothed, often reddish. Flowers in hollow-stalked umbels, each with 4–10 flowers; petals 5, pink-purple to dark purple, upper 2 petals slightly larger, with dark red veins; faintly scented. All parts emit a strong scent when crushed. Root and leaves formally used medicinally. Introduced into cultivation in England in 1690, it is the main ancestor of the popular Regal pelargoniums of horticulture. Stem cuttings are quick-and-easy to root. Leaf and root extensively used in traditional medicine.

Jo Onderstall

Pelargonium incrassatum

Geraniaceae   Spring

Namaqualand beauty

T'knytjie

Perennial herb, up to 300 mm high with a turnip-shaped tuber; occurring in karroid vegetation, usually among granitic rocks. Leaves in a basal rosette, ovate to narrowly ovate in outline, deeply lobed into scalloped segments, with silvery hairs. Flowers in an umbel at the end of a long, erect, unbranched stalk; petals 5, bright pinkish purple, upper 2 much larger than the rest. The brilliantly coloured flowers can be spotted from afar among the colourful spring-flowering annuals of Namaqualand; pollinated by *Prosoeca peringueyi*, a long-tongued fly. Plants deciduous during the dry season (summer). Peeled tubers cooked in milk or baked under hot ash are considered a delicacy by the local people. An attractive pot plant; plants should be kept dry during the dormant season.

Braam van Wyk

Pelargonium luridum

Geraniaceae — Spring–Summer

Stalk-flowered pelargonium — Grasveld-rabas

Perennial herb, up to 1 m high, with a tuber; occurring in grassland and bushveld. Leaves in a basal rosette, usually covered with long hairs, extremely variable, even on the same plant: lamina varies from slightly lobed to deeply dissected, the segments thread-like in some forms. Flowers in an umbel of 5–60 flowers at the end of a long, slender, erect, unbranched stalk; petals 5, ± equal and without blotches, very variable in colour: white, cream, creamy pale green, salmon pink or greenish yellow. A conspicuous species because of its tall inflorescences that sway in the slightest breeze above the grasses. An infusion of the tuber, which is pinkish red inside, is a popular traditional remedy against diarrhoea and dysentery; pharmacological effects may be due to the presence of tannins.

Braam van Wyk & Sasa Malan

Pelargonium peltatum

Geraniaceae — Spring

Ivy-leaved pelargonium — Kolsuring

A herbaceous, ± hairless perennial creeper; occurring in thicket and along forest margins. Leaves ± rounded in outline, bluntly 5-angled or lobed, ± shield-shaped with the stalk attached slightly to the inside of the margin (peltate), or cordate with stalk inserted at the margin (*P. lateripes*), sometimes with a dark-reddish marking centrally on the upper surface; margin smooth. Flowers in stalked umbels of 2–9 flowers; petals 5, mauve or pinkish mauve to pale pink, upper two slightly larger with darker markings; sepals often tinged dull red. Leaves with a sour-tasting sap used as an antiseptic for sore throats. Petals yield a blue pigment once used in paintings. The ancestor of many cultivars of 'ivy-leaved geraniums' grown in gardens worldwide; introduced to Holland in 1700 and Britain in 1774.

Braam van Wyk

Rhodohypoxis baurii

Hypoxidaceae   Spring–Summer

Red star

Rooisterretjie

A small perennial herb, up to 150 mm high, with a tuberous rhizome; occurring in grassland, usually in damp and rocky places. Leaves spreading, sparsely covered with long hairs. Flowers on long, slender stalks; perianth with 3 large and 3 small, ± horizontally spreading lobes, usually pink, red or white, faintly scented; anthers hidden by the upward bending of the 3 inner perianth lobes. The most widespread member of the genus; floral colour very variable, even in the same colony. Plants often grow in dense stands, creating colourful patches. Attractive garden plant, best suited for areas with a cool, moist climate. *R. milloides* has hairless leaves, or very nearly so. There are ± 6 species of *Rhodohypoxis*, all confined to the central Drakensberg and surrounding areas.

Braam van Wyk

Antholyza ringens (= *Babiana ringens*)

Iridaceae   Winter–Spring

Rat's tail

Rotstert

Erect perennial, up to 400 mm high, with a deep-seated corm; occurring mainly in fynbos and strandveld, often in sandy soil. Leaves stiff and erect, strongly pleated. Flowers on a ± horizontal side branch towards base of main inflorescence axis, irregular; perianth strongly 2-lipped, with protruding stamens held within a tube formed by the upper lip, bright red. Flowers conspicuous and can be seen from a distance; pollinated by sunbirds. Upper part of main inflorescence axis remains sterile and bare, hence the common names. As with several local members of the Iridaceae the corms, known as *uintjies*, are edible; they are used in a variety of dishes. *A. plicata* (= *Babiana thunbergii*) from Namaqualand grows up to 1 m high, and the inflorescence has several side branches.

John Manning

Crocosmia paniculata (= *Curtonus paniculatus*)

Iridaceae   Summer

Pleated leaves

Waaierlelie

Robust perennial, up to 2.5 m high, sprouting annually from a corm; occurring as dense stands in grassland, usually in marshy places and where water collects along roadsides. Leaves in a fan, stiff, erect, deeply pleated, ± 800 × 60 mm. Flowers borne well above the leaves, arranged on several well-spaced, horizontally spreading and ± zigzagged side branches towards the end of a tall, erect flowering stalk; corolla tubular, strongly 2-lipped with protruding stamens, dark brick red. Flowers pollinated by sunbirds, which use the sturdy side branches of the inflorescence as a perch. As in many bird-pollinated flowers, they are scentless; birds generally have a poorly developed sense of smell. Used in traditional medicine. Attractive, cold-hardy garden plant; dormant during winter.

Braam van Wyk

Dierama spp.

Iridaceae   Mainly Spring–Summer

Hairbells

Grasklokkies

Evergreen, grass-like perennial herbs with corms; occurring in grassland. Flowers borne on tall, slender stems that divide at the top into a number of usually pendulous flowering branchlets on thin, wiry, flexible stalks; perianth bell-shaped, very dark red to pale yellow or whitish, but most often shades of pink or mauve, each perianth lobe (tepal) usually marked with a ± diamond-shaped 'eye' inside at the base. The slender inflorescences sway in the slightest breeze. About 37 species of *Dierama* occur in the region; distribution map shows total range of the genus. Correct species identification often requires expert knowledge, the morphology of the bracts being of great importance. Accompanying photograph is of *D. tyrium* on Mariepskop in Mpumalanga.

Braam van Wyk

Gladiolus oppositiflorus

Iridaceae   Summer

Salmon gladiolus
Transkeiswaardlelie

Erect perennial herb, up to 1.5 m high, with a corm; occurring in grassland, especially along foothills and slopes of the southern Drakensberg Escarpment. Leaves arranged in a fan, narrowly sword-shaped, with the midrib and margins thickened and yellow, reaching at least to the base of the spike, with short hairs. Flowers usually 7–15, borne in an erect spike, ± 2-ranked, large (mostly 80–110 mm long), salmon to pale pink or mauve, lower 3 tepals with a reddish or purple stripe in the lower half. A most attractive plant, cultivated in England as early as 1837. One of the principal species originally used to breed the large-flowered gladiolus hybrids, which are extensively grown as summer cut flowers and garden plants throughout the world today.

Tom de Waal

Watsonia borbonica (= *W. pyramidata*)

Iridaceae   Spring–Summer

Pyramid watsonia
Pienksuurknol

A clump-forming perennial, up to 2 m high, with a corm; occurring in fynbos, usually in well-drained sandy soils on rocky sandstone slopes. Leaves 20–40 mm wide, glossy-green. Flowers in an erect, branched spike, the main axis with up to 20 flowers; perianth irregular; tepals spreading outwards, with free part 26–36 mm long, pale to deep pink to light purple, with a white streak at the base of each tepal; anthers violet. A conspicuous species of the Cape Peninsula; flowers profusely after fire. Flowers are bee-pollinated. A popular garden plant; combines well with blue-flowered *Aristea major*. Plants die back and are dormant during summer. *W. rogersii*, with which it is often associated, has smaller flowers (tepals 22–25 mm long) and narrower leaves (5–10 mm wide).

Colin Paterson-Jones

Watsonia densiflora

Iridaceae | Summer | Natal watsonia / Natalse watsonia

Erect, clump-forming perennial herb, up to 1.2 m high, with a corm; occurring in grassland, especially along the coast. Leaves grey-green. Flowers ± 30–42, densely arranged in erect spikes; axis with densely packed, dry, brownish, overlapping bracts; perianth bright pink with a darker pink line in middle of each tepal. A conspicuous and very floriferous species; often growing in extensive colonies. Requires plenty of water when grown in gardens. Plants are dormant during winter. Corms edible, also used in traditional medicine. *W. confusa* has pale blue-green leaves and spikes of 15–30 flowers; tends to occur more inland. *W. lepida*, centred in and around the Maluti and central Drakensberg Mountains, usually grows as a solitary plant and is much smaller (up to 650 mm high).

Watsonia strubeniae

Iridaceae | Summer | Graskop watsonia / Graskopse watsonia

Erect perennial herb, up to 1 m high, with a corm; occurring in grassland, often as scattered plants in large stands on mountain slopes. Leaves 4 or 5 in a fan, reaching to about the base of the spike. Flowers in long, slender, 2- or 3-branched, erect spikes; main spike has 25–35 flowers, side ones with fewer flowers; flowers pointing in opposite directions (2-ranked), irregular, funnel-shaped; tepals pale pink, each with a darker median stripe, free part 17–19 mm long. A most handsome plant that creates splashes of pink that contrast vividly with its green grassland habitat; threatened by commercial afforestation. Closely related to *W. transvaalensis* from the Graskop-Wolkberg area, that has larger flowers (tepals 20–25 mm long) and a usually unbranched inflorescence.

97

Ballota africana (= *Marrubium africanum*) Cat herb

Lamiaceae   Autumn–Spring   Kattekruid

Soft, greyish, hairy perennial; occurring in fynbos and karroid vegetation, often along watercourses. Stems 4-angled. Leaves opposite, rounded or ovate, densely covered with simple and star-shaped hairs; base cordate to rounded; margin irregularly toothed; venation conspicuously sunken above. Flowers in round clusters above each leaf pair; calyx funnel-shaped, persistent in fruit; corolla tubular, 2-lipped, pink or purple. Strongly scented when crushed. A very popular traditional medicine for a variety of ailments, including measles, colds, influenza, respiratory problems, heart trouble, piles and arthritis. Administered in the form of an infusion (¼ cup fresh leaves and a few flower whorls, steeped in a cup of boiling water for about 5 minutes) or a brandy tincture.

Ben-Erik van Wyk

Hemizygia transvaalensis   Large hemizygia

Lamiaceae   Spring–Summer   Groot-hemizygia

Erect, bushy shrublet, up to 1 m high, with many annual stems from a woody perennial rootstock; occurring in grassland, often among rocks. Leaves opposite, sessile or with a very short stalk; blade usually ovate to broadly ovate 15–40 × 8–22 mm, dull green above and below. Flowers produced towards ends of shoots, in whorls of 3–6 flowers at each node; corolla tubular, 2-lipped, 18–22 mm long, whitish to mauve or lilac-pink; bracts very conspicuous, 12–24 × 4–10 mm, bright pink. Plants flower profusely after a fire; most of the colour being produced by the showy bracts rather than the flowers. Leaves and stems somewhat sticky and strongly aromatic when crushed. *H. thorncroftii*, mainly from the Barberton area, has flowers with a 14–16 mm-long corolla.

Braam van Wyk

Syncolostemon densiflorus

Lamiaceae Summer–Autumn

Pink plume
Pienkpluim

Martin von Fintel

Sparingly-branched perennial shrub, up to 2.5 m high; occurring in grassland; usually along forest margins or in rocky places. Stems with short, white, hairs. Leaves opposite; blade ovate or broadly elliptic to rounded, gland-dotted, with rough hairs. Flowers densely clustered in branched, terminal inflorescences, in groups of 4–6 flowers; calyx reddish mauve; corolla 2-lipped, 18–23 mm long, pale to bright pink, rarely whitish; stamens protruding. Most parts strongly aromatic when crushed; used in traditional medicine. Plants do not burn easily; forests may receive some protection against grassland fires from the dense stands often found along their margins – a type of natural firebreak. A very showy plant but difficult to maintain in gardens. *S. rotundifolius* (Pondoland) has flowers in clusters of two.

Aloe arborescens

Liliaceae Autumn–Winter

Krantz aloe
Kransaalwyn

Braam van Wyk

Much-branched succulent shrub or small tree, up to 3 m high; occurring in high-rainfall grassland and forest areas, usually in rocky places. Leaves in terminal somewhat obliquely disposed rosettes, dull greyish or bluish green; spineless on both surfaces; margin with pale teeth. Flowers usually in unbranched, erect spikes, 200–300 mm long, 2–4 per rosette; scarlet, orange, pink or yellow. A decorative garden plant, easily propagated from cuttings or truncheons; probably the most widely cultivated aloe in the world. It is also grown as a live fence around cattle kraals. Pulp from leaves is used medicinally, with proven success against X-ray burns. Closely related to *A. mutabilis* (Witwatersrand to Pietersburg), a smaller plant with bicoloured racemes (buds red, open flowers yellow).

Aloe claviflora

Liliaceae   Spring

Kraal aloe
Kraalaalwyn

Ben-Erik van Wyk

Perennial succulent, with leaves in a ± asymmetrical rosette; stems absent or very short; occurring in karroid vegetation, in dense groups or circular patches on hill slopes or flat stony areas. Leaves greyish green, rough-textured, with a few spines on the lower surface towards the tip; margin with brown spines. Inflorescences produced at an angle, often almost horizontal to the ground; flowers club-shaped, arranged in densely flowered, bicoloured racemes, buds and young flowers bright red, older ones yellow fading to white; perianth 30–40 mm long, ± 10 mm wide. Common names refer to the peculiar growth habit of the plants; older plants in the centre of a clump die back, with the younger ones remaining in a circle on the periphery, thus forming a ring or *kraal*.

Aloe davyana (= *A. greatheadii* var. *davyana*)

Liliaceae   Winter

Common spotted aloe
Gewone bontaalwyn

Braam van Wyk

Stemless succulent with leaves in a basal rosette; occurring in grassland in bushveld, often in stony places. Leaves with upper surface green and dotted with many whitish spots, lower surface whitish green and ± without spots; margin with sharp, brown spines. Inflorescence up to 1 m high, with up to 5 branches; racemes ± densely congested, conical, 150–200 mm long; flowers with perianth usually pale pink, constricted above the ovary. Plants tend to proliferate in overgrazed areas. An effective soil binder that can by used to stabilise soil banks and disturbed areas. Leaf pulp used medicinally to treat burns, sores and wounds. *A. greatheadii* has shorter racemes (± 90 mm). *A. transvaalensis*, a summer-flowering species, has reddish flowers in well-spaced racemes.

Aloe maculata (= *A. saponaria*)

Liliaceae   Summer–Spring

Soap aloe

Seepaalwyn

Succulent which has leaves in a rather open, flat, basal rosette; stemless, or with a short, erect stem less than 1 m high; occurring in coastal and montane grassland, usually in large colonies; solitary or in clumps of several individuals. Leaves spotted above and below; tip dry, twisted; margin with brown teeth. Inflorescence with up to 6 branches; flowers in dense, flat-topped racemes, yellow, orange or red. A widespread and variable species; however, the usually flat-topped racemes are very characteristic, making this one of the easier spotted aloes to identify. Widely used in traditional medicine to treat wounds and other ailments. Leaf sap formerly used in the tanning of hides. Cut leaves yield a copious flow of sap, which froths like soap when the cut ends are rubbed together, hence the common names.

Tom de Waal

Aloe striata

Liliaceae   Winter–Spring

Coral aloe

Gladdeblaaraalwyn

Succulent which has leaves in a basal rosette, stemless, or with a short, creeping stem; occurring in thicket and karroid vegetation, usually in large colonies. Leaves pale blue-green, often tinged with red, distinctly striate, unspotted; margin spineless, with a soft, reddish edge. Inflorescence a branched, flat-topped raceme, up to 1 m high; buds and flowers coral-red, ± drooping; perianth 25–35 mm long, with a basal swelling. One of the very few species of aloe with spineless leaves. An attractive garden plant. A cross with *A. maculata* is probably the most widely cultivated aloe hybrid (hybrid retains pink marginal border). Related to *A. karasbergensis* (Northern Cape and southern Namibia), which has conspicuously green-veined leaves and a much-branched, pyramidal panicle.

Braam van Wyk

Gloriosa superba

Flame lily

Liliaceae   Summer   Vlamlelie

A perennial herb with climbing annual shoots from an underground tuber; occurring in thicket, along forest margins and on coastal dunes. Leaves strap-shaped, tapering to a coiled tendril, glossy green. Flowers large and conspicuous, downward-facing; petals strongly reflexed, yellow, red-and-yellow, red or deep pink, margin undulate; style bent at a right angle to the ovary. Capsules green, with bright red seed. Plants show great variety in flower size and colour. Plants poisonous, containing colchicine and related compounds. Colchicine has anticancer properties, but is too toxic for human use. Widely utilised in traditional medicine, but such practices should be discouraged because the plant is implicated in human deaths and developmental abnormalities in newborn babies.

Piet van Wyk–Agfa

Veltheimia capensis

Sand lily

Liliaceae   Autumn–Winter   Sandlelie

An erect perennial with a partly-exposed bulb; occurring in karroid vegetation, fynbos and strandveld. Leaves in a basal rosette, spreading, greyish green, hairless; margin usually undulate. Flowers in a dense raceme at the end of a sturdy, spotted, erect stalk, drooping, cylindrical, various shades of mottled pink, tipped green, with black, pear-shaped seeds. Fruit a capsule, large, membranous; stamens exserted a short way from mouth of tube. Easily grown in gardens, but frost-sensitive; requires sandy soil, and a sunny position and dry conditions when dormant in summer. Bulbs should be planted with at least one-third above ground. *V. bracteata* (mainly Eastern Cape) is the only other member in the genus. It is ± evergreen and prefers shady conditions; bulb is completely below ground.

Braam van Wyk

Hibiscus marlothianus

Limestone hibiscus

Malvaceae   Summer–Autumn   Kalksteen-hibiskus

Braam van Wyk

A low-growing perennial herb, with a woody rootstock; occurring in grassland, bushveld and karroid vegetation, often on limestone or alkaline soils. Leaves deeply divided, often 3-lobed, with unevenly toothed margins, sparingly covered with star-shaped hairs; stalk ± the same length as central lobe of leaf. Flowers pale to dark pink or whitish, with a dark purple centre; calyx of two dissimilar whorls, sepals of lower whorl ± half the length of those in the upper whorl. Pollinated by honeybees. Flowers similar to that of *H. microcarpus* (red form), which has long, narrow, unlobed leaves. Also resembles the pink form of *H. aethiopicus*, which has oval leaves with a blunt tip. There are more than 50 species of *Hibiscus* in the region, most with yellow, pink or red flowers.

Hibiscus praeteritus

Slender red hibiscus

Malvaceae   Summer   Yl-rooihibiskus

Braam van Wyk

An erect, sparsely-branched perennial shrublet, up to 2.5 m high; occurring in bushveld, often along roadsides or river banks. Stems green, with coarse star-shaped hairs. Leaves alternate, ovate, ± 20–30 × 10–20 mm, sparsely dotted with star-shaped hairs; margin coarsely toothed; stalks slender, 5–10 mm long. Flowers solitary, on long, slender stalks in the axils of the upper leaves; lower calyx whorl with 10 narrow lobes; corolla 30 mm in diameter, with 5 bright scarlet petals; staminal column twisted about 90° with 5 long style branches. Although the flowers are relatively small, their brilliant coloration makes them very conspicuous. A number of rather similar looking scarlet-flowered *Hibiscus* species occur in the region. Expert knowledge is, however, required to distinguish among them.

Radyera urens

Malvaceae   Summer–Autumn

Karoo pumpkin
Pampoenbossie

Perennial herb with robust, trailing stems; occurring in arid karroid vegetation types, often along roadsides. Leaves rounded, large (up to 120 mm in diameter), grey-green and densely covered with star-shaped hairs, prominently veined below, erect on long stalks; base heart-shaped; margin crinkled. Flowers borne in leaf axils, often shaded by the leaves; petals deep red; stamens yellowish red, fused into a column around the style. Fruit a capsule opening with five valves. A member of the hibiscus family, but with growth form and leaves superficially very similar to that of a pumpkin. An infusion of the root is used as a remedy against piles. Plants are not grazed by livestock. The genus, which has only this single species, is named after the eminent South African botanists, Dr R.A. Dyer.

Dissotis canescens

Melastomataceae   Summer

Pink marsh dissotis
Pienkkalwerbossie

Perennial herb, up to 1.5 m high, sprouting annually from an extensive underground rootstock; occurring in grassland and bushveld, usually in marshy situations and along streams. Stems 4-angled, reddish brown. Leaves opposite, with 3–5 prominent veins from the base. Flowers in clusters near ends of stems, 35–45 mm in diameter, bright pink. Plants often grow in dense stands in marshes, resulting in mass displays of brilliant pink during flowering. Flowers are 'buzz pollinated'; when anthers are vibrated by a bee, the fine, powdery pollen is forcefully discharged through a tiny apical pore. Used medicinally to treat dysentery, diarrhoea and hangovers. Attractive plant for water features in gardens; requires soil rich in organic material, and full sun.

Nymania capensis

Meliaceae — Winter–Spring

Chinese lantern
Klapperbos

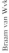

Rigid shrub or small tree, up to 3 m high; occurring in hot, semidesert areas, often along watercourses. Leaves ± linear, leathery, with dense hairs to hairless, unpleasantly scented when crushed. Flowers axillary, solitary, greenish pink to dark pink or scarlet, becoming bell-shaped with age. Fruit a papery, inflated capsule, creamy pink to bright reddish pink, with a silvery sheen. Shoots and leaves very bitter due to limonoids (chemicals which deter herbivorous insects). Flowers have two strategies to ensure pollination. First they are tubular with lots of nectar for attracting sunbirds, then they change to bell-shaped and display the polliniferous stamens, to attract honeybees. The fruit is wind-dispersed. Plants from the Little Karoo and Eastern Cape larger and less hairy than those from the Northern Cape.

Carpobrotus acinaciformis

Mesembryanthemaceae — Spring

Pink sour fig
Pienksuurvy

Mat-forming perennial succulent, with robust trailing stems; occurring in fynbos and strandveld, usually on coastal dunes. Stems ± winged. Leaves opposite, 3-angled, greyish green, often tinged with red. Flowers large (70–100 mm in diameter), with short stalks, and numerous rose-purple petals. Fruit fleshy, oval, yellowish brown, turning ± leathery when old. Fresh leaves are chewed as a cure for sore throats; sap from the leaves is used as lotion for burns and blue-bottle stings. Fruit of this and other species used to make a delicious jam, but preparing it requires some skill. It is naturalised in parts of Italy. *C. edulis* has yellow flowers. Five other species occur in South Africa, often on sandy areas along the coast. Generic name derived from the Greek *karpos* = a fruit + *brotus* = edible.

Drosanthemum hispidum

Mesembryanthemaceae   Spring

Common dew vygie
Gewone douvygie

Spreading, succulent perennial, up to 200 mm high; occurring in karroid vegetation, often as extensive stands in flat, sandy plains. Leaves opposite, cylindrical, covered by swollen water-storage cells that glisten in sunlight. Flowers up to 30 mm in diameter, with numerous petals, bright pink. Flowers open around midday and close by evening. As in most other members of the family, the dry seed capsules open in response to moisture. They have a complicated internal structure and function as splash cups; kinetic energy from rain drops is used to forcefully expel seed from the capsules. With almost 2 000 native species, Mesembryanthemaceae (mesembs or vygies) is by far the most important family of succulents in the region. Most species are found in the Succulent Karoo Biome.

Colin Paterson-Jones

Commicarpus pentandrus

Nyctaginaceae   Summer

Cerise stars
Veldpatat

A perennial herb with annual, trailing stems, sprouting from a large tuberous rootstock; occurring in grassland, bushveld and karroid vegetation, often along roadsides. Leaves opposite, widely spaced, ovate, ± 40 mm in diameter. Flowers in whorls at tips of slender, erect stalks, borne all along the trailing stems; corolla funnel-shaped, bright pink. Fruit with ± 5 large, sticky, purplish brown glands. An unmistakable species that often forms large, brilliantly coloured patches flat on the ground. Plants grow very old and some of the larger underground tubers may be more than a century old. Tubers edible; they are either cooked or baked under hot ash. Grazed by livestock. Seeds dispersed by animals; glandular fruit adheres to clothing and animal hides.

Braam van Wyk

Oxalis purpurea

Oxalidaceae   Autumn–Spring

Pink sorrel

Pienksuuring

Low-growing perennial herb, up to 150 mm high, with tuberous bulbs; occurring in fynbos and disturbed places, often in large colonies. Leaves in a basal rosette, palmately compound, with 3 rounded leaflets. Flowers solitary, erect, on slender stalks; corolla with lobes spirally twisted, bright pink with a yellow centre. A native plant that often occurs as a weed on lawns in the southwestern Cape. Flowers open in response to bright sunlight. The leaves have an acid-taste and are used as a vegetable, to flavour food, or as a replacement for salt. Tubers are peeled, cooked and served like potatoes. The region is a major centre of diversity for *Oxalis*, with more than 130 species in the Cape Floristic Region alone. Many native members have considerable horticultural potential.

Braam van Wyk

Ceratotheca triloba

Pedaliaceae   Summer

Wild foxglove

Vingerhoedblom

Erect annual herb, up to 2 m high, most parts covered with fine hairs; occurring mainly in bushveld, usually along roadsides and in disturbed places. Leaves opposite, ± deeply divided into 3 lobes; margin bluntly toothed. Flowers borne on short stalks in axils of leaves along upper portion of stems, drooping; corolla pale pink to mauve, lower lip with purplish stripes, and fine hairs. Fruit a hairy capsule with 2 horns at the tip. Unpleasantly scented when crushed. A tea made from the leaves is used in traditional medicine, especially for intestinal disorders. Together with other ingredients, it makes an effective insect-repellent spray, especially for aphids on roses and pot plants. Its use on vegetables is not recommended, because of its fetid odour.

Braam van Wyk & Sasa Malan

Dicerocaryum senecioides

Pedaliaceae   Summer–Autumn

Devil's thorn

Elandsdoring

Mat-forming perennial herb, with long, trailing, annual stems from a woody rootstock; occurring in bushveld, often along roadsides or in sandy places. Leaves grey-green above, powdery white below; margin deeply lobed. Flowers borne all along the stem, on slender, erect stalks; corolla irregular, pink, with darker nectar guides. Fruit a flattened, elliptic and very hard disc lying flat on the ground, with two very sharp, erect spikes on the upper surface. Fresh plant material crushed in water yields a mucilaginous mass formerly used as soap substitute. Leaves rubbed with water between the hands yield a soapy lather; formerly also used in rural areas as a lubricant for childbirth. The spiny fruit is able to penetrate hoofs and feet causing considerable pain.

Braam van Wyk

Pterodiscus speciosus

Pedaliaceae   Summer

Water potato

Ruiterblom

Semi-succulent perennial herb, sprouting annually from a thick, fleshy tuber; occurring in grassland and bushveld. Leaves linear-lanceolate, greyish green; ± fleshy; margin toothed. Flowers ± solitary in leaf axils, with short stalks; corolla broadly funnel-shaped, weakly irregular, dark pink, outside of floral tube with minute whitish dots. Fruit with four longitudinal wings. Tubers edible when fresh. Also used to brew a beer; tubers are peeled, dried, pounded, mixed with cold water and honey and allowed to ferment. Two dark, purple-black glands (extrafloral nectaries) are located at the base of each flower stalk. These structures secrete a sweet substance and are eagerly visited by ants. Apparently the presence of ants deters other herbivorous insects that may damage the plant.

Braam van Wyk

Sesamum triphyllum

Pedaliaceae   Spring–Summer

Wild sesame

Wildesesam

Braam van Wyk

An erect, sparsely branched annual or short-lived perennial herb, up to 1.5 m high; occurring in grassland and bushveld, often along roadsides and in disturbed places. Leaves opposite, simple to deeply palmately divided, unpleasantly scented; margin sometimes faintly toothed. Flowers solitary, axillary, with short stalks; corolla brownish pink, dark pink to bluish pink. Fruit a cylindrical capsule with a pointed tip, splitting in half when ripe (hence expression 'open sesame'). Flower stalks each subtended by small black glands (extrafloral nectaries); these attract ants, the presence of which deters insect herbivores. Seeds edible and rich in oil. Sesame seed, from *S. orientale*, is the oldest grown oil seed (since ± 3500–3050 BC). *S. alatum* usually has brighter pink flowers and simple leaves.

Saltera sarcocolla

Penaeaceae   All year

Fly bush

Vlieëbos

John Manning

Sparsely-branched, rather untidy perennial shrublet, up to 1 m high; occurring in fynbos, usually in sandy soils derived from sandstone. Leaves opposite, rounded, leathery, overlapping, 4-ranked. Flowers clustered at ends of stems, surrounded by sticky, bract-like leaves; corolla usually pink, often with white markings, sticky. Small insects get stuck in the sticky secretions of the bracts and flowers, hence the common names. Penaeaceae is one of eight plant families that are endemic or near-endemic to the Cape Floristic Region. *Sonderothamnus speciosus* (mainly Klein River Mountains near Hermanus) has leaves with a thickened, dark-coloured tip; they are very neatly arranged, mainly along the upper parts of stems. Flowers surrounded by fringed bracts, neither being sticky.

Melinis repens (= *Rhynchelytrum repens*)

Poaceae   Summer–Autumn

Natal red top

Natalse rooipluim

An annual or short-lived perennial grass, growing in tufts; occurring mainly in grassland, bushveld and karroid vegetation, often in disturbed places, especially abundant along roadsides and in fallow fields. Leaves bright green, with expanded blades and a prominent midrib. Inflorescence a much-branched panicle; spikelets hairy, various shades of pink, fading to white. One of the most common and widespread grasses in the region. A beautiful sight when growing in dense stands on the shoulders of roads. Palatable pioneer or sub-climax grass; plays an important role in stabilising disturbed soil. Used in flower arrangements. *M. nerviglumis*, a perennial with more compact silvery-pink inflorescences, grows on rocky hillsides; it has thread-like (rolled), blue-green leaves.

Braam van Wyk & Sasa Malan

Nylandtia spinosa (= *Mundia spinosa*)

Polygalaceae   Autumn–Spring

Tortoise berry

Skilpadbessie

A much-branched, rigid shrub, up to 4 m high; young twigs spine-tipped; occurring in fynbos, renosterveld and strandveld; usually in sandy soils. Branches short, robust; side branches usually transformed into short spines. Leaves very small, thick. Flowers produced along branches, irregular, purple, pink or white; petals 3, united at the base, lower one keel-like, enclosing the stamens, with a lobed appendage below its tip. Fruit a globose berry, shiny and red when ripe. Berries edible, but with an astringent taste; eaten by birds, tortoises and people. Fruit, leaves and young twigs used medicinally for the treatment of tuberculosis and stomach disorders. *N. scoparia* has elongated, slender branches, side branches not transformed into short spines and leaves that are usually absent at flowering.

John Manning

Polygala virgata

Polygalaceae   All year

Purple broom

Bloukappies

A slender, single-stemmed shrub, up to 3 m tall, sparsely branched in the upper third; occurring in grassland and along forest margins. Leaves narrowly elliptic, ± 20–90 × 1–20 mm, with short stalks, often dropping before flowering. Flowers in long, terminal racemes, pink to purplish pink; wings (enlarged sepals) with dark purplish veins; keel with a brush-like appendage. Widely cultivated in gardens for its attractive flowers and extended flowering period. Flowers superficially similar to those of members of the pea family (Fabaceae). Known as 'keel flowers', they are functionally adapted for bee pollination. In its search for nectar, the visiting bee depresses the movable keel petal, whereupon the sexual organs are released and touch the insect, either depositing or picking up pollen, thus effecting pollination.

Braam van Wyk

Mimetes cucullatus

Proteaceae   All year

Common pagoda

Rooistompie

Shrub, up to 2 m high, with many erect stems from a large rootstock; occurring in fynbos. Leaves oblong-elliptic, hairless; apex with 1–3 teeth, each tipped by a reddish gland. Flowers in large, cylindrical inflorescences at the ends of stems, topped by a crown of flat, red, reduced leaves; flowers subtended and clasped from above by orange-red leaves; perianth segments white, hairy. The showy part of the inflorescence is provided by the colourful leaves interspersed between the flowers. Seed with a fleshy appendage; collected and taken underground by ants. Plants rapidly resprout after fire. This is the most widespread of the 13 species of *Mimetes*, a genus endemic to the Cape Floristic Region. Most of the species have a very local distribution and at least one is already considered extinct.

Colin Paterson-Jones

111

Agathosma ovata

Rutaceae — All year

Oval-leaved buchu — Basterboegoe

Tony Abbott

A bushy shrublet, up to 500 mm high, sprouting from a perennial rootstock; occurring in grassland and fynbos. Leaves oval to roundish, ± 15 mm long, dull green above, shiny bright green below; margin recurved. Flowers borne among leaves towards ends of branches, ± 10 mm in diameter; petals 5, free, pink to white. A wide-ranging and very variable species. A member of the citrus-family, most parts have a strong citrus-scent when crushed. Used medicinally to treat nervous disorders and other ailments. About 140 species of *Agathosma* occur in the region, most of them confined to the Cape Floristic Region. Leaves of *A. betulina* and *A. crenulata* are the main sources of the buchu of commerce, a popular traditional remedy against kidney and urinary-tract infections.

Cycnium racemosum

Scrophulariaceae — Summer–Autumn

Large pink ink plant — Berginkplant

Martin von Fintel

An erect usually un-branched perennial herb, up to 800 mm high; occurring in grassland, usually in rocky places. Stems ± 4-angled, often tinged with purple. Leaves opposite below, alternate higher up the stem, ± 80 x 20 mm, rough; margin toothed, purplish red. Flowers in terminal racemes, alternate or in pairs; corolla large, ± 60 mm in diameter, usually deep pink with a whitish centre, sweetly scented. A very conspicuous and most attractive hemiparasite. Known host plants include various grasses and species of *Acalypha*. Bruised flowers turn black, hence the common names. Used medicinally as an emetic and as a general painkiller. Generic name derived from the Latin *cygnus* (= a swan) in reference to the white flowers of *C. adonense*, a low growing grassland species.

Diascia namaquensis

Scrophulariaceae   Winter–Spring

Namaqualand twinspur

Namakwalandse horinkie

Braam van Wyk

Erect annual herb, up to 400 mm high; occurring in karroid vegetation and fynbos, usually in sandy places. Leaves opposite; margin toothed. Flowers solitary at the ends of erect stalks, irregular, pink to purple-red, with two prominent spurs or sacs on the lower back surface of the corolla. The spurs contain glandular hairs on the inside near the tips. These hairs secrete oil, which is collected by solitary bees of the genus *Rediviva*. As a bee alights on the flower, it inserts its long forelegs into the two spurs. Once inside the spurs, oil is absorbed by special hairs on the bee's legs. In the process pollen is transferred from the flower to the visiting bee; the bee then effects pollination when it visits the next flower. Forelegs of the bees often closely match the length of the spurs of their host plant.

Graderia scabra

Scrophulariaceae   Spring

Wild penstemon

Wilde penstemon

Tom de Waal

A tufted herb with annual shoots from a perennial rootstock, up to 600 mm high; occurring in grassland. Leaves alternate, stalkless, overlapping, ± 50 x 15 mm, roughly hairy; margin smooth, with a few coarse teeth. Flowers in leafy terminal racemes; corolla irregular, pink, rarely white, outer surface with short hairs; filaments hairy towards base only. Fruit a capsule, many-seeded. Flowers profusely after late winter or early spring fires. Used in traditional medicine for various ailments. *G. subintegra* is very common in Highveld grassland; it has leaves that are not rough to the touch and filaments with hairs along almost their entire length. The name *Graderia* is an anagram of *Gerardia*, the name of a genus confined to the New World and presently known as *Agalinis*.

113

Phygelius aequalis

Scrophulariaceae   Summer–Autumn

River bells

Rivierklokkie

Herbaceous perennial shrublet, up to 1 m high; occurring along stream banks in montane grassland. Stems 4-angled. Leaves opposite, oval, 75–100 × 40 mm, dark green above, pale green below, soft-textured; margin toothed; stalk ± 25 mm long. Flowers in a rather compact terminal panicle, drooping; corolla ± 40 mm long, pale pinkish red, lobes ± subequal, outlined in deep red, yellow on the inside; stamens and style exserted. Fruit a capsule. Flowers are pollinated by sunbirds. Used in traditional medicine. A cold-hardy plant suitable for moist sites in temperate gardens. *P. capensis* is the only other species in the genus. It has drooping, coral-red flowers in lax panicles; these are borne on stalks that are sharply bent so that the flowers point towards the main inflorescence axis.

Tom de Waal

Striga elegans

Scrophulariaceae   Summer–Autumn

Large witchweed

Grootrooiblom

Slender, erect herb; stem simple or rarely slightly branched; occurring in grassland. Leaves opposite, stiff, erect, covered with minute, rough hairs. Flowers borne towards tips of stems; corolla irregular, 12–20 mm long, 2-lipped, upper lip not much shorter than the lower lip, scarlet on inner and orange-yellow on outer surface. Fruit a capsule, many-seeded. A root parasite of grasses, although rarely attacking crop plants. It is classified as a hemiparasite because the plant contains chlorophyll and is therefore partly self-sustaining. *S. asiatica* has smaller flowers (12 mm long) with the upper lip of the corolla much shorter than the lower. It is often found as a parasite on maize, sorghum and sugar cane. Cultural methods of control are employed to eradicate plants from crops.

Braam van Wyk & Sasa Malan

Hermannia grandiflora

Bell bush

Sterculiaceae — Summer–Autumn — Ouma-se-kappie

Bossie Kotzé

A much-branched perennial shrublet, with a roundish shape, up to 1 m high; occurring in karroid vegetation. Leaves alternate or in tufts, elliptic, 2–15 × 2–4 mm; margin coarsely toothed. Flowers borne in groups of 2 on long, slender stalks near branch tips, all facing downwards; petals 5, free, pale red, twisted. Flowers are usually produced in profusion and may cover the whole bush, resulting in striking patches of colour. Drought-resistant, palatable and well grazed by livestock; presence of plants indicates veld in good condition. Superficially very similar to *H. stricta,* which also produces red flowers in profusion. It has larger, solitary flowers on stalks rarely longer than 12 mm, and has a more restricted distribution in the hot, arid areas along the lower reaches of the Orange River.

*Lantana camara

Lantana

Verbenaceae — Summer–Winter — Lantana

Braam van Wyk

A much-branched, perennial shrub; invading grassland, bushveld and forest margins, often occurring in disturbed places under and among trees. Stems 4-angled, with scattered, recurved prickles. Leaves opposite, with rough hairs, unpleasantly scented when crushed. Flowers congested in flat-topped heads, predominant colour very variable, including pink, yellow, orange or orange-brown. Fruit fleshy, globose, shiny black. A native of Central and South America; cultivated for ornament and hedging. Poisonous to livestock. This is a declared weed in South Africa. Flowers in the centre of the inflorescence open first and usually change colour as they fade. This colour change probably signals to pollinating insects which flowers have been pollinated, and which have not.

115

Barleria obtusa

Acanthaceae   Autumn   Bush violet

                                                         Bosviooltjie

Sprawling perennial shrublet, which is rather untidy in appearance; occurring in grassland, thicket and bushveld, often in semishade and associated with rocky outcrops or clusters of trees and shrubs. Most parts with soft, silky hairs. Leaves opposite, oval, ± 50 × 30 mm, dark green, with very short stalks. Flowers in clusters of 1–4, mainly towards ends of branchlets, slightly irregular; petals usually blue, rarely white or pink, with the throat darker than the lobes; anthers deep blue. Fruit a flattened capsule, with 1–4 seeds. A very floriferous species widely grown in gardens; easily cultivated from cuttings. Flowers attract butterflies that probably act as pollinators. Dry capsules dehisce explosively when moistened to release the flattened seeds. Browsed by livestock and game.

Braam van Wyk

Agapanthus inapertus

Alliaceae   Summer   Drooping agapanthus

                                                        Drakensberg-bloulelie

Deciduous perennial herb, up to 1.5 m high, with a rhizome and numerous fleshy roots; occurring in high-rainfall grassland or scrub, often associated with rocky outcrops, forest margins or stream banks. Leaves bluish green, basally overlapping and forming a stem-like structure. Flowers in umbels, deep blue to almost purple-black; perianth segments tubular, not (or only slightly) spreading; stalks erect in bud, becoming drooping or pendulous in open flowers. An aggregate species with many different forms. Floral colour may vary from blue to purple-black in the same population. An attractive garden plant, but less frequently grown than the next species. The generic name is derived from the Greek *agape* = love and *anthos* = flower; *inapertus* means 'closed', alluding to the tubular flowers.

Braam van Wyk

Agapanthus praecox

Alliaceae   Summer

Common agapanthus

Gewone bloulelie

Evergreen perennial herb, up to 1.5 m high, with a rhizome and numerous fleshy roots; occurring in high-rainfall grassland, often along forest margins or in rocky places. Leaves dark green, not aggregated into a stem-like structure at the base. Flowers in umbels, pale blue or rarely white, with a short tube and spreading perianth segments; stalks erect or spreading. Fruit a capsule; seed numerous, flat, winged, shiny black. A very popular garden plant throughout the world. In traditional medicine a decoction of the rhizome and roots, or water in which a plant was grown, are widely used by women before and after childbirth. Crude extracts of the plant have a proven effect on the contraction of the uterus wall. *Agapanthus* is a genus of about ten species, all confined to southern Africa.

Berkheya purpurea

Asteraceae   Summer–Autumn

Purple berkheya

Persdisseldoring

A stout, very spiny perennial herb, up to 1 m high, with a single, central stem; occurring in damp, high altitude montane grassland, often in large colonies. Stem with spiny, longitudinal wings. Leaves mainly in a basal rosette, dark green with rough hairs above and white felt below; margin coarsely toothed, with sharp spines. Flower heads (see page 140) with ray florets pale to deep mauve, rarely white, disc florets purple. *Berkheya* is named after the Dutch botanist, Jan le Francq van Berkhey (1729–1812). Most of the about 75 species are confined to South Africa. Flower heads in the genus are commonly yellow, *B. purpurea* being the only member with purple flowers. These very beautiful plants are virtually impossible to handle because of all the spines.

Braam van Wyk

Darrel Plowes

*Cichorium intybus

Asteraceae   Spring–Summer   Chicory / Sigorei

Erect perennial herb, up to 1 m high, with a fleshy taproot; occurring near areas of human habitation, especially in moist places. Basal leaves large, with the margin irregularly toothed and lobed. Flower heads (see page 140) comprising only strap-like ray florets, clear pale blue, borne in clusters of 2 or 3 on well-branched, ± leafless stems. A native of Asia and Europe. Introduced as an agricultural crop and now naturalised in many parts of the region. Flowers open in the morning and close by midday. The leaves are cooked as a spinach, but at least two changes of water are required to remove bitter principles. Root used as a diluent of coffee, a coffee substitute, an adulterant and to extract locust antifeedants (chemicals which deter locusts). Leaf, stem and root are also widely used in traditional medicine.

Felicia filifolia

Asteraceae   Spring   Fine-leaved felicia / Persbergdraaibos

Erect much-branched ± evergreen perennial shrublet, up to 1 m high; occurring in grassland and karroid shrubland. Stems pale creamy brown. Leaves in tufts, needle-like. Flower heads (see page 140) borne in profusion along the length of the stem, aromatic; ray florets mauve to white; disc florets yellow. Four subspecies are recognised. Subspecies *filifolia* is the most widespread and often proliferates in overgrazed grassland. Although not very palatable to livestock (apparently poisonous in some areas), it imparts a characteristic flavour to meat. Plants are very attractive when in flower and are occasionally grown in gardens. Subspecies *schaeferi* (*kleingombos*), a smaller plant, is much more palatable to livestock; it is mainly confined to the winter-rainfall Karoo (Succulent Karoo Biome).

Vernonia fastigiata

Asteraceae   Spring–Summer

Narrow-leaved vernonia

Smalblaarbitterbossie

Annual or short-lived perennial herb, which is usually much-branched and twiggy; occurring mainly in bushveld and associated grassland, often a weed in disturbed places, particularly along roadsides. Leaves sparsely present, stalkless, ± 40 × 4 mm; margin smooth. Flower heads (see page 140) produced at tips of stems, ± 20 mm in diameter, purple, consisting of disc florets only; bracts long, bristle-tipped, recurved and woolly. Plants are extended bloomers and flower heads are produced virtually throughout the growing season. The flower heads are extremely popular among a great variety of butterflies and the presence of the plants can be recognised at a distance from the mere aggregation of these insects. In *V. poskeana* the involucral bracts are usually not spreading or recurved.

Braam van Wyk

Vernonia natalensis

Asteraceae   Spring

Silver vernonia

Silverbitterbossie

Silvery, erect many-stemmed perennial herb, up to 1 m high, with a woody root-stock; occurring in grassland. Leaves with short stalk (up to 2 mm) or stalkless, long and narrow, 35–60 × 4–15 mm; base tapering; both surfaces with silvery silky hairs. Flower heads (see page 140) in a cluster at end of each stem, comprising disc florets only, purple; bracts surrounding head with long, curved tips. Plants often occur in large colonies; easily recognised from a distance by their silvery colour. Various parts of the plant are used in traditional medicine to treat coughs, malaria and many other ailments. Leaves and roots are used by the Zulu people as charms against lightning. May be confused with *V. oligocephala* (see next entry), a species with the leaves rounded at the base and ± hairless above.

Braam van Wyk & Sasa Malan

Vernonia oligocephala
Bicoloured-leaved vernonia

Asteraceae | Spring | Bitterbossie

Braam van Wyk & Sasa Malan

A robust or slender, erect perennial shrublet, up to 1 m high, with few to many stems sprouting from a woody rootstock; occurring in grassland. Leaves almost stalkless, oval to ovate; base rounded; apex often ending abruptly in a sharp point; dull green and ± hairless above, densely covered with silvery hairs below. Flower heads (see page 140) about 10 mm in diameter, numerous, clustered together in ± flat-topped groups at ends of shoots, dark purple. A tea prepared from the leaves is a popular and tried remedy against mild forms of diabetes. Also used as a disinfectant and to treat many other ailments. The tea is extremely bitter (hence the Afrikaans name) – a taste probably imparted by the presence of sesquiterpenoid lactones, compounds with antibacterial and antifungal properties.

*Echium plantagineum
Purple bugloss

Boraginaceae | Spring | Pers-echium

Riaan de Villiers

Annual or biennial herb, with 1 – many flowering stems, up to 0.8 m high; most parts with soft, appressed hairs; occurring along roadsides, in waste ground and as a weed of cultivation. Basal leaves ovate to oblanceolate; side veins prominent above and below. Upper stem leaves stalkless; base heart-shaped. Flowers broadly funnel-shaped, blue or deep purplish blue; stamens 5, of which 2 protrude. A native of western Europe, southwestern Britain and the Mediterranean region. Rather similar to *E. vulgare*, a native of Europe, which is also naturalised in the region. The latter occurs mainly along the southern and central Drakensberg. Its basal leaves are narrowly lanceolate, the side veins are not prominent and the stem leaves have tapering bases; flowers with 4 stamens protruding.

Lobostemon fruticosus

Boraginaceae   Spring

Eight-day healing bush

Agtdaegeneesbos

Photo credit: Braam van Wyk

Soft-wooded silvery, laxly branched perennial shrub, up to 2.5 m high; occurring in fynbos, locally abundant in sandy places on flats and mountain slopes. Leaves strapshaped, 15–60 × 5–12 mm, with dense hairs, aromatic when crushed; margin smooth. Flowers in clusters near ends of branches; corolla funnel-shaped, in various subtle shades of blue and pink, even in the same plant, rarely white, with short hairs. Early colonists at the Cape used an infusion of the leaves to treat body sores and other skin eruptions such as ringworm. The salve was thought to bring about healing within eight days, hence the common names. Distantly related to comfrey and borage, two popular Eurasian medicinal plants of the same family, with similar wound-healing properties.

Heliophila coronopifolia

Brassicaceae   Spring

Blue sporrie

Blou-sporrie

Photo credit: Braam van Wyk

Erect annual herb, up to 0.6 m high, often freely branched above; occurring in fynbos and renosterveld. Leaves simple or pinnately lobed, with a greyish bloom; lobes up to 3 mm wide. Flowers bright blue with a white or pale greenish yellow centre. Fruit 30–90 × 1.3–2 mm, constricted at regular intervals between the seed, giving a beaded appearance. There are about 70 species of *Heliophila* in the region, most with vivid blue flowers, the rest white- and yellow-flowered (common among spring flowers in Namaqualand). Flowers tend mainly to open on warm sunny days, hence the name *Heliophila*, which means 'sun-lover'. Although the individual flowers are extremely dainty, plants often grow in dense masses, resulting in spectacular shows of colour.

121

Commelina livingstonii

Commelinaceae Summer

Livingston's blue commelina

Gewone blouselblom

Perennial herb with spreading, branched stems from a woody crown, usually hairy; occurring in grassland and bushveld. Leaves narrowly ovate, ± 70 × 20 mm, folded along midrib, greyish green. Flowering spathes clustered at tips of stems, ± stalkless, folded with margins joined at the base, outer surface finely ribbed, with bristly hairs; flowers opening one at a time, pale to dark blue. The boat-shaped spathes are filled with a clear, tasteless and somewhat viscous liquid that covers the young, developing flower buds. When a bud is ready to open, it pulls from the liquid, emerges from the spathe and unfolds its very delicate petals in early morning, only to fade by noon. There are about ten species of *Commelina* with blue or mauve flowers in the region.

Cyanotis speciosa (= *C. nodiflora*)

Commelinaceae Spring–Summer

Doll's powderpuff

Bloupoeierkwassie

Perennial herb that sprouts annually from a short rhizome, up to 400 mm high; occurring in grassland. Leaves clustered in a basal rosette, ± channelled, lower surface with short, ± erect hairs. Flowers on erect inflorescences, in clusters of 1–3, blue, purple, mauve or pink; stamens very hairy, creating the impression of a powderpuff and providing most of the colour, anthers white. Flowers open in the morning and fade by midday. Floral colour varies between different parts of its range, usually more bluish towards the west and more pinkish towards the east. Roots used for medicinal and magical purposes. *Cyanotis lapidosa* has leaves with appressed hairs on both surfaces and ± reclining inflorescences. It grows in colonies on rocky areas.

Streptocarpus primulifolius
Gesneriaceae

Primula-leaved streptocarpus

Summer–Autumn Primulablaar-streptocarpus

Perennial herb with a stout, horizontal rhizome; occurring in the understorey of forest, often on rock faces. Leaves in a basal rosette, up to 450 × 110 mm, hairy. Inflorescence erect, up to 260 mm high, with 1–4 flowers; corolla large, 65–90 mm long, pale bluish violet with broad reddish purple nectar guides. Closely related to *S. formosus*, which has a yellow corolla-tube-floor with purple-brown lines (coastal forests of Transkei and southern KwaZulu-Natal). About 50 species of *Streptocarpus* occur in the region, most associated with forest. *S. wendlandii* is one of several rarities in the group. It has a single large leaf up to 500 × 400 mm, the latter being dark green above and deep purplish red below; plants die after flowering. It is confined to the Ngoye Forest in KwaZulu-Natal.

Auriol Batten

Aristea major (= *A. thyrsiflora*)
Iridaceae

Giant aristea

Spring

Blousuurknol

A robust evergreen perennial, up to 1.5 m high, sprouting from a rhizome and forming dense clumps; occurring in fynbos, usually in marshy places on mountain slopes. Leaves erect, rigid, long and strap-shaped, bluish green, leathery. Flowers borne in dense clusters on long inflorescences, regular, bright blue, with a satiny lustre. Fruit a capsule. An attractive species, even when not in flower; widely cultivated in gardens, even thriving in semishade. Attractively combined with yellow *Wachendorfia thyrsiflora* (page 44) and pink *Watsonia borbonica* (page 96). Plants should be kept moist throughout the year. Individual flowers are short-lived, they open in the morning and shrivel-up after midday, the tepals twisting as they fade. Fortunately, new buds open continuously over a long period.

Gerald Cubitt

123

Moraea polystachya

Iridaceae   Autumn–Winter

Karoo blue tulp

Karoobloutulp

Erect perennial, up to 0.8 m high, with a corm; occurring in arid karroid shrub-land, on stony/shale flats or on rocky slopes, often proliferating in overgrazed areas. Leaves 3–5, long and narrow, channelled to almost flat. Flowers violet to pale blue; tepals 6, outer 3 with yellow to orange nectar guides. Plants often occur in dense stands, imparting a blue colour to the veld when in flower. Although the individual flowers last only a single day, the flowering period may continue for up to six weeks. Extremely poisonous to cattle and sheep, with death occurring 24–48 hours after ingestion of the plants. Newly introduced or hungry livestock are most at risk. Animals raised on tulp-infested veld learn to avoid it. The toxic principles are cardio-active glycosides (bufadienolides).

Robert Archer

Moraea tripetala

Iridaceae   Spring

Dainty moraea

Blou-uintjie

Slender, erect perennial, up to 0.5 m high, with a corm; occurring in arid karroid shrubland, fynbos and renosterveld, both on clay and sandy soils. Leaf solitary or rarely 2, long and narrow. Flowers usually pale to dark blue to purple, with only the outer 3 of the 6 tepals well developed. An easily recognised species on account of the apparently absent but actually very reduced inner tepals. Among the major colour variants are plants with attractive yellow or sometimes pinkish flowers. It is probably pollinated by small carpenter bees. Of the about 120 species of *Moraea*, no less than 65 are restricted to the winter-rainfall area of South Africa. All are characterised by iris-like flowers, which usually are short-lived, lasting less than a day; some may open in the late afternoon and fade shortly after sunset.

Colin Paterson-Jones

Plectranthus ecklonii

Lamiaceae   Summer–Autumn

Large spur-flower bush

Persmuishondblaar

A perennial, soft-wooded and much-branched shrub, up to 2.5 m high, occurring in the understorey of forest. Leaves 60–170 x 40–100 mm, with very few hairs; venation prominently raised below; margin toothed. Flowers borne in profusion in branched terminal panicles; corolla purplish blue, narrow, up to 20 mm long, gradually expanding to the throat, not expanded at the base. An attractive plant for shady gardens; pink and white cultivars are popular. The leaves, which have an unpleasant odour when crushed, are used traditionally to treat headaches and hayfever. About 45 species of *Plectranthus* occur in the region, most of them confined to the high-rainfall eastern and northern parts. The group is well known for its aromatic leaves, attractive flowers and preference for shady habitats.

Braam van Wyk

Pycnostachys urticifolia

Lamiaceae   Autumn–Winter

Large hedgehog bush

Groot-ystervarksalie

Sparsely branched, soft-wooded perennial shrub, up to 3 m high; occurring in grassland and bushveld, usually in marshy places, along stream banks or forest margins. Leaves broadly ovate, distinctly stalked; margin toothed. Flowers in spikes at tips of branches, dark blue or rarely white; corolla with lower lip large and boat-shaped; calyx persistent in fruit, the pointed lobes developing into sharp, reddish spines. Flowers open in succession, with rarely more than three rows open at a time. Occasionally planted in gardens, but plants are frost-sensitive and not very showy. The common names refer to the spiny inflorescences. *P. reticulata* has essentially stalkless, linear to lanceolate leaves; it is more widespread in the region. Generic name from the Greek *pyknos* = dense + *stachys* = a spike.

Braam van Wyk

Salvia africana-caerulea (= *S. africana*)

Lamiaceae   Spring–Summer

Cape blue sage

Kaapse blousalie

Sparingly branched, perennial shrub, up to 2 m high; occurring in coastal fynbos and on rocky slopes. Leaves greyish green, obovate-elliptic to broadly obovate, hairy. Flowers in whorls of 2–6 among persistent bracts, 5–12 of these whorls arranged in spike-like inflorescences; corolla pale blue to bluish purple or pinkish, lower lip with a paler blue margin and white to yellowish in the centre. Most parts strongly aromatic when crushed. One of the first plants used by the Dutch at the Cape as a household medicine. A bitter-tasting tea prepared from the leaves is popular as a treatment for colds, flu and various other ailments; sugar, honey or lemon juice may be added. Plants are easily propagated by cuttings. *S. chamelaeagnea* has 2-flowered whorls arranged in large panicles, and deciduous bracts.

John Manning

Tetradenia riparia (= *Iboza riparia*)

Lamiaceae   Winter

Iboza

Watersalie

Robust, deciduous, somewhat succulent, perennial shrub, up to about 3 m high; occurring in bushveld, usually on rocky hillsides and along streams in relatively frost-free areas. Stems stout, brittle, 4-angled when young. Leaves velvety; margin toothed. Inflorescences large, spreading, diffusely branched, the ultimate branchlets spike-like; flowers very small, mauve or rarely white. Most parts are strongly lavender-scented when crushed. Flowering takes place when plants are leafless in winter, creating the impression of a mauve mist. Plants are either male (illustrated) or female, with the female spikes being more compact. An attractive garden plant for frost-free areas; easily grown from cuttings. Widely used in traditional medicine. 'Iboza' is a Zulu vernacular name for the species.

Braam van Wyk

Scilla natalensis

Liliaceae   Spring–Summer

Large blue scilla

Blouslangkop

Deciduous perennial herb, up to 1 m high, sprouting annually from a large bulb located half-above ground; occurring singly or as colonies in moist grassland, often in rocky places. Leaves erect, up to 500 mm long, grey-green. Flowers distinctly stalked, borne in a raceme on a sturdy stalk up to 1 m high, usually produced with the new leaves, pale to deep purplish blue. A very variable species, although some of the smaller plants currently classified under this name probably belong to different species. The bulb is extensively used in traditional medicine to treat various ailments, including sprains, boils, sores, female infertility and internal tumours. An attractive, frost-resistant garden plant; for best results bulbs should be planted partly above ground and left undisturbed for many years.

Ben-Erik van Wyk

Lobelia coronopifolia

Lobeliaceae   All year

Coastal lobelia

Kus-lobelia

Perennial herb, up to 0.6 m high, sprouting from a woody rootstock; occurring in coastal grassland, usually in sandy soil. Leaves in a basal rosette, 20–45 × 1–3 mm; margin toothed. Flowers sparsely arranged in terminal racemes; corolla ± 25 mm long, purplish blue, irregular, with three large lower lobes and two small, recurved upper lobes, the latter resembling horns. All parts of the plant contain a milky latex. Flowers are visited by honeybees and butterflies. The leaf is used in traditional medicine; some members of the genus contain lobeline, an alkaloid with similar but less potent properties than nicotine. Propagated from seed or cuttings, it makes an attractive and hardy garden plant. The genus is named after Matthias de l'Obel (1538–1616), a famous Flemish nobleman, physician and botanist.

Tony Abbott

Lobelia erinus (= *L. nuda*)

Lobeliaceae   Spring

Wild lobelia

Wilde-lobelia

Small, slender, erect annual herb; occurring in grassland and fallow fields, usually in moist places. Leaves concentrated towards base, sometimes ± in a basal rosette; blade usually 4–20 mm wide, narrowing into a stalk-like base or with stalks up to 15 mm long. Flowers borne on slender stalks in a branched inflorescence, pale blue; base of lower lip with a large, white blotch; throat yellow. Plants often form extensive stands in seasonally wet places in grassland. When these stands flower simultaneously in early spring, the resultant large patches of blue create an extremely realistic illusion of pools of water. Powdered roots and leaves are mixed with a little water and sniffed to clear a blocked nose. About 80 species of *Lobelia* are native to the region.

Rosemary Williams

Dissotis princeps

Melastomataceae   Summer–Winter

Purple dissotis

Perskalwerbos

A robust perennial herb or a much-branched shrub, up to 3 m high, most parts with short, bristly hairs; occurring in grassland and bushveld, usually in swampy places or along streams. Leaves opposite, usually lanceolate to ovate-lanceolate; lamina with 5–7 prominent veins from the base. Flowers in sparse or compact terminal clusters; petals ± 25 × 20 mm, lilac to dark purple or violet, rarely white; anthers unequal, purple. Each anther has a tiny pore at the tip. For the dry, powdery pollen to be released, the anthers need to be vibrated ('buzzed') by a bee at a specific frequency. The vibration causes the pollen grains to resonate inside the anther, resulting in their forceful release from the pore. The root is used in traditional medicine; formerly also as a famine food.

Braam van Wyk

Nymphaea nouchali (= *N. caerulea*; *N. capensis*)   Blue waterlily

Nymphaeaceae   All year   Blouwaterlelie

Aquatic herb with floating leaves and a tuberous rhizome; occurring in standing fresh-water pools, pans and dams, or in slow-moving streams. Leaves with undersurface purple to green; margin toothed or smooth. Flowers pale blue to mauve, with a centre of yellow stamens; sweetly scented, especially at night. Tubers are boiled or roasted by rural people as a vegetable; they are spongy and rather tasteless. The seed, well pounded to meal, may be cooked as porridge. Occurs throughout tropical Africa, as far north as Egypt; the stem, tuber, flower, fruit and seed are also widely used for medicinal and magical purposes. Plants contain various alkaloids. Commonly cultivated in garden ponds. *N. lotus* is the only other waterlily native to the region; it has creamy white flowers.

Tony Pooley

---

*Limonium sinuatum   Statice

Plumbaginaceae   Spring–Autumn   Papierblom

Erect, bushy, short-lived perennial, up to 400 mm high; occurring in disturbed sites in fynbos, renosterveld and karroid shrubland, especially along roadsides. Stems longitudinally winged. Leaves oblanceolate, deeply pinnately lobed, hairy. Flowers in showy clusters at the tips of branches; calyx funnel-shaped, dry and membranous, purple; petals white. A native of the Mediterranean region. Popular in dried-flower arrangements because the flowers retain their form and colour for many months after gathering. Cultivars are available with calyces (sing. calyx) in shades of pink, red, orange, yellow, blue and lavender. *Limonium* is a genus of some 300 species of cosmopolitan distribution, especially Mediterranean; most are found on open seashores or salt marshes.

Braam van Wyk

Plumbago auriculata

Plumbaginaceae   Spring–Autumn

Plumbago

Kaapse bloublommetjie

Braam van Wyk

Scrambling, much-branched shrub, up to 2.5 m high; occurring in thicket and bushveld, often in rocky places. Leaves oblong or wedge-shaped, lower surface sometimes with numerous tiny white spots (calcium salts excreted by glands); stalk short, slightly winged, with two small lobes ('ears') at the base. Flowers in terminal racemes; petals pale blue, each with a purple midrib; calyx with sticky hairs; anthers blue. A popular garden ornamental worldwide; makes an excellent flowering hedge. White- and dark-blue-flowered cultivars available. Effectively combined in gardens with the yellow-flowered form of *Tecomaria capensis* (page 63), which flowers at the same time. Various parts used in traditional medicine. *P. zeylanica* is a smaller plant with white flowers.

Conostomium natalense

Rubiaceae   Summer

Wild pentas

Wildepentas

Braam van Wyk

Erect, herbaceous to slightly woody perennial shrublet, up to 1 m high; occurring in grassland and associated bushveld, often on forest margins or in disturbed places. Leaves opposite, lanceolate, 30–75 × 6–25 mm; midrib conspicuously sunken above; base ± rounded; stalk very short; stipules present, interpetiolar. Flowers in terminal heads, surrounded by leafy bracts; corolla tube up to 18 mm long, pale blue or lilac, rarely white; calyx lobes long and narrow, persisting in fruit. *Conostomium* has flowers with 4 petals, a useful character to distinguish it from *Pentanisia*, a rather similar-looking genus that has 5 petals. Parts of the plant are used by the Zulu people in traditional medicine, whereas the roots are utilised as love charms and for magical purposes by the Venda people.

Pentanisia prunelloides

Rubiaceae   Spring–Summer

Hairy-leaved pentanisia

Sooibrandbossie

Herbaceous perennial shrublet, up to 0.5 m high, with trailing to erect annual stems from a thick, tuberous rootstock; occurring in grassland. Leaves opposite, extremely variable in size, usually ± hairy. Flowers congested in dense terminal heads, pale to deep purplish blue. The herbaceous nature of the above-ground parts belies the true age of the plants; judged from the great size of their underground tubers, many are estimated to be several decades old. Both the Afrikaans common name (meaning 'heartburn shrublet') and the Zulu/Xhosa name, *Icishamlilo* (meaning 'that which puts out the fire') refer to the use of the plant to treat heartburn; a small piece of fresh root is chewed and swallowed. Tubers are also extensively used for various other ailments. *P. angustifolia* has ± hairless leaves.

Wally Menne

Aptosimum procumbens (= *A. depressum*)

Scrophulariaceae   Summer

Karoo violet

Karooviooltjie

Mat-forming perennial herb, up to 1.5 m in diameter, that sprouts annually from a woody rootstock; occurring in grassland and karroid shrubland. Stems prostrate, radiating from the root, leafy throughout. Leaves narrowly or broadly obovate; stalk much shorter than the lamina. Flowers produced all along the stems, often in profusion, irregular, deep blue or violet, rarely maroon, with white markings at the throat. Very attractive when in full bloom, otherwise a rather insignificant plant. Used medicinally for bladder and other ailments in man and for *krimpsiekte* in sheep. *A. spinescens*, with very similar flowers, is an erect, branched shrublet with needle-like, spine-tipped leaves that are densely crowded along the stems. It is confined to the Nama-Karoo and Succulent Karoo Biomes.

Bossie Kotzé

131

Jamesbrittenia macrantha (= *Sutera macrantha*) Sekhukhune wild phlox
Scrophulariaceae   Summer   Sekhukhune-wildefloks

Braam van Wyk

Perennial shrublet, up to 1 m high; occurring in bushveld and associated grassland, usually on soils rich in heavy metals derived from ultramafic rocks, often along roadsides. Leaves almost hairless, with a few scattered glistening glands; margin toothed. Flowers solitary in axils of upper leaves, which are reduced; corolla with lobes lilac to deep violet-mauve, throat yellowish green. One of several plant species endemic to Sekhukhuneland. An attractive but relatively unknown plant similar to *J. grandiflora*, a species often cultivated and easily distinguished by its leaves, which are hairy and densely covered in glistening glands, particularly on the lower surface. It occurs from Mount Sheba to Barberton along the Drakensberg Escarpment, and in the Eastern Highlands of Swaziland.

Selago serrata   Cape blue haze
Scrophulariaceae   Spring–Summer   Kaapse blouaarbos

John Manning

Erect or sprawling, evergreen perennial shrublet, up to 1 m high; occurring in fynbos, usually among rocks on mountain slopes. Stems stout, angular. Leaves densely arranged, oval, 5–10 mm wide, thick and leathery, tips slightly recurved, hairless; margin distinctly toothed. Flowers very small, blue or mauve; borne in dense, round-topped heads, up to 120 mm in diameter at the ends of the stems. The individual units of the inflorescences elongate at fruiting time. This is the most showy member of the genus in the Western Cape; bought flowers may be used for arrangements. In cultivation it does best in the winter-rainfall area. *S. spuria* also has round-topped inflorescences (though often smaller) and clearly toothed leaves, but the latter are only 1–3 mm wide.

132

Tetraselago wilmsii (= *Selago wilmsii*)

Scrophulariaceae   Summer–Autumn

Transvaal blue haze

Transvaalblouaarbos

Evergreen perennial shrublet, up to 0.5 m high, with several erect, usually unbranched stems; occurring in grassland, usually in rocky places. Leaves ± 20 × 3–5 mm. Flowers very small, blue, mauve or rarely white, densely arranged in small racemes of 10–14 flowers, the latter aggregated into terminal, slightly round-topped inflorescences up to ± 60 mm in diameter. In *T. nelsonii* the partial inflorescences are ± rounded heads. *T. natalensis* (KwaZulu-Natal) has the partial inflorescences more loosely arranged, each with 10–45 flowers, and the leaves are slightly longer (± 30 × 3 mm). *Tetraselago* is superficially very similar to *Selago* and the two genera appear similar when in flower. However, the fruit in the former is a tiny dehiscent capsule, and in the latter, four indehiscent nutlets.

Braam van Wyk

Walafrida geniculata

Scrophulariaceae   Summer–Winter

Waterfinder

Persaarbos

Perennial shrublet, up to 0.5 m high, old growth woody; occurring in karroid vegetation types, usually in low-lying parts. Leaves bright green, strap-shaped, up to 20 × 2 mm; margin smooth. Flowers densely arranged in 50–100 mm long spikes at branch tips, lilac to purple, occasionally white, very small, each with 2 upward- and 3 downward-pointing petals. Plants may be female (relatively rare) or bisexual (illustrated), the inflorescences of the latter being denser and somewhat rounder. Very palatable to livestock, drought-resistant and resprouts quickly after grazing, or even after light rain. Its presence is indicative of good veld condition. Easily confused with *Selago albida*, which is strongly scented, tends to have more rounded inflorescences and prefers rocky mountains and ridges.

Bossie Kotzé

133

Solanum panduriforme

Solanaceae   Spring–Summer

Poison apple

Gifappel

Perennial shrublet, up to 0.5 m high, sprouting from an extensive system of underground stems; occurring in grassland and bushveld. Stems usually without prickles. Leaves lanceolate, both surfaces rather similar in colour; margin smooth. Flowers solitary or in small axillary clusters; petals mauve; anthers with very short filaments, coherent to form a central cone, bright yellow. Fruit round, ± 20 mm in diameter, yellow. The root and fruit are widely used in traditional medicine. Both the green and ripe fruit are poisonous. All native species of *Solanum* have anthers with minute pores at the tip. Bees release the pollen grains from the pores by rapid vibration of their thoracic muscles as they hang from the anther cone (so-called 'buzz pollination').

Xerophyta retinervis

Velloziaceae   Spring

Monkey's tail

Bobbejaanstert

A deciduous perennial, with stout, erect, sometimes sparsely branched stems; occurring on rocky ridges in grassland and bushveld. Stems densely covered with a thick mantle of fire-charred, closely packed, persistent leaf bases, and have numerous densely packed roots (stem tissue dies off at an early stage) inside. Leaves grass-like, keeled, in terminal tufts. Flowers deep to pale mauve or white, borne in abundance on slender stalks amongst the leaves, especially after fire. The persistent leaf bases provide excellent protection against veld fires. Plants are very slow-growing and large ones are estimated to be well over a hundred years old. Attempts to grow these interesting plants in gardens have failed. The root is used in traditional medicine to treat asthma.

*Verbena aristigera (= *V. tenuisecta*)

| Verbenaceae | Spring–Summer | Fine-leaved verbena
Fynblaarverbena |

Braam van Wyk

Short-lived, sprawl-ing herb, up to 200 mm high; occurring in disturbed places, particularly along roadsides. Leaves deeply dissected, both surfaces hairy; base stem-clasping. Flowers in dense, flat-topped, terminal spikes, the latter elongating considerably as new flowers are produced at the ends; petals bright mauve, fading to blue, occasionally white, tips distinctly notched. A native of South America; widely grown as a ground cover in gardens. Naturalised throughout the region, but not a serious weed of cultivation, and control measures are rarely required. *Verbena*, a genus of ± 200 species, is mostly confined to the tropical and temperate parts of North and South America, with a few in Europe and Asia; there are no species native to South Africa. Many species are used in traditional medicine.

*Verbena bonariensis

| Verbenaceae | Summer | Wild verbena
Blouwaterbossie |

Braam van Wyk

An erect, sparsely branched annual, up to 2 m high, with rough hairs; occurring in grassland and disturbed sites, especially in wet places. Stems tough and fibrous. Leaves opposite, stalkless and ± clasping at the base. Flowers in branched, flat-topped, congested inflorescences, very small, purple. A native of South America. The flowers are popular with butterflies and other insects. Inflorescences are dried, coloured and used in dried-flower arrangements. *V. brasiliensis* (from South America) has leaves that are distinctly stalked with the base narrowly tapering; its inflorescences tend to be slender and smaller. *V. officinalis* (from Europe), a smaller plant, has ± well-spaced flowers on long, narrow, terminal spikes, and lower leaves that are deeply lobed or pinnately divided.

Asclepias albens (= *A. affinis*)

Asclepiadaceae   Summer

Cartwheels
Wawielmelkbos

Braam van Wyk & Sasa Malan

A perennial herb, with a tuberous rootstock; occurring in grassland. Most parts with milky latex. Leaves ovate, with course hairs. Flowers distinctly stalked, clustered into a terminal, flat-topped head, which is turned sideways; corolla lobes reflex, white, greenish or cream, often tinged with pink; corona lobes ± square, opening upwards, green or yellowish. Flowers (see page 140) highly specialised. Stamens and style are fused together to form a central column. Five greenish cups (corona) secrete nectar. Pollen grains united into pollinia and connected in pairs (5 per flower) to a wishbone-shaped structure, all concealed except for a tiny blackish gland. Pollinia are withdrawn when the legs or mouthparts of visiting insects are guided towards the gland by special grooves on the column.

Pachycarpus campanulatus

Asclepiadaceae   Summer

Fairy-bell pachycarpus
Feeklokkie-pachycarpus

Martin von Fintel

A slender, erect perennial herb, up to 600 mm high, sprouting annually from a tuber; occurring in grassland. Most parts with milky latex. Stems 1 or 2, ± coarse haired. Leaves opposite, erect, spreading, very narrowly linear to lanceolate, 64–165 x 2–10 mm; margin rolled downward. Flowers in a terminal umbel with 3–14 flowers, usually drooping; corolla cup- or bell-shaped, 10–15 mm long, pale green or dull cream-green, becoming cream-brown in old flowers. Plants flower most profusely in regularly burned grassland. The generic name is derived from the Greek, *pachys* (= thick) and *carpus* (= fruit), referring to the large inflated fruit of some of the species (not this one). At least 24 species are known from the region, all confined to summer-rainfall grassland.

Erica sessiliflora

Ericaceae   Autumn–Spring

Green heath
Groenheide

Erect, robust evergreen shrub, up to 2 m high; occurring in fynbos, usually in marshy areas, or between rocks where there is an increase in water runoff. Stems densely covered in leaves, hairless. Leaves needle-like, 4–14 mm long. Flowers tightly arranged in spikes near the ends of branches; corolla tubular, 16–30 mm long, pale green; anthers not protruding; sepals fleshy. Easy to identify, even if not in flower. The fleshy sepals are persistent and increase in size during fruiting. They acquire a reddish tinge and, together with the fruit, may remain on the plant for many years. Fruiting heads reminiscent of a cancerous deformity or a fungal infection; responsible for the Afrikaans name *Mielieheide*, because it resembles a maize cob. Persistent fruits release their seeds only after fire, a trait known as serotiny.

Colin Paterson-Jones

Eucomis autumnalis

Liliaceae   Summer

Common pineapple flower
Gewone wildepynappel

A deciduous herb with a bulb; occurring in grassland, especially in moist places or on rocky ridges. Leaves in a basal rosette, strap-shaped, 150–550 × 40–130 mm, hairless, often with a wavy margin. Inflorescence stalk erect, ending in a tuft of green leaf-like bracts above the densely packed flowers; perianth segments pale yellow-green to whitish. The inflorescence has the appearance of a pineapple, hence the common names. The bulbs are extensively used in traditional medicine to treat a variety of ailments, including urinary-tract and lung diseases, stomach ache, fevers, biliousness, blood disorders and venereal diseases. Over-collecting for the herbal trade is a serious threat to natural populations of this species. A genus of at least ten species, all confined to southern Africa.

Braam van Wyk & Sasa Malan

Synonyms are supplied for some terms, and are given in brackets at the end of the definition. Also see the line drawings on pages 7 and 140.

Annual a plant that completes its life cycle from germination to seeding and death within one year.

apical pore a tiny opening at the tip of the pollen bearing anther.

appressed lying close to or pressed flat against a surface or structure, as the hairs on certain leaves.

berry a many-seeded fleshy fruit with a soft outer portion and the seeds embedded in the fleshy or pulpy tissue (e.g. the tomato).

biennial a plant that grows and develops in the first year, and fruits and seeds in the second; living for two growing seasons.

bract a usually small, leaf-like structure, in the axil of which arises a flower or a branch of an inflorescence.

bulb a swollen underground organ comprising a short, disc-like stem with fleshy and tightly overlapping leaf bases (e.g. the onion).

capsule a dry fruit produced by an ovary comprising two or more united carpels and usually opening by slits or pores.

corm a shortened (compressed) and swollen underground stem that produces leaves at the top, enclosed by dry, fibrous leaf bases; characteristic of many Iridaceae.

deciduous shedding leaves at the end of the growing season.

dehiscent opening when mature, as in anthers or fruit.

discoid having only disc florets (e.g. some members of Asteraceae).

dissected deeply divided or irregularly cut into many segments.

distal towards the tip, or the end of an organ (e.g. root, stem or leaf).

enantiomorphy showing 'handedness'; with structures (e.g. keel; style; stamens) twisted or bent towards either the left or the right.

enantiostyly a phenomenon in which the style is bent to the right in some flowers (or plants) and to the left in other flowers (or plants); flowers show 'handedness'.

endemic strictly confined to a specific region or substrate.

epiphyte a plant that grows on another plant but is not parasitic on it.

evergreen retaining green leaves throughout the year, even during winter months.

exserted projecting beyond surrounding parts, as stamens protruding from a corolla; not included.

fallow said of land left uncultivated after being ploughed and seeded at an earlier time.

2-fid dividing into two lobes or parts.

floriferous bearing many flowers.

flower head a dense inflorescence of many small, crowded, often stalkless flowers (florets) at the end of a common stalk; ± spherical or dish-shaped.

globose spherical, rounded.

forb a non-grassy herbaceous plant.

hemiparasite a parasitic plant that contains chlorophyll and is therefore partly self-sustaining, as in many Scrophulariaceae. Holoparasites on the other hand lack chlorophyll and are entirely dependent on the host for nourishment.

herb (herbaceous) a plant that does not develop persistent woody tissue above ground and either dies at the end of the growing season or overwinters by means of underground organs (e.g. rhizomes, bulbs, corms).

heterostylous with styles of different lengths in flowers of plants in the same species.

incised with the margin deeply cut.

indigenous a plant occurring naturally in an area and not introduced from elsewhere (= native).

inflorescence any arrangement of more than one flower; the flowering portion of a plant, e.g. head, spike, panicle, raceme.

interpetiolar between the leaf stalks, as an interpetiolar stipule that extends from the base of one leafstalk across the stem to the base of the stalk of the opposite leaf (e.g. in many Rubiaceae).

involucre a whorl of bracts subtending a flower or flower cluster.

karroid Karoo-like; used to describe vegetation types typical or reminiscent of the semidesert Karoo region of South Africa, namely a sparse vegetation dominated by dwarf, perennial shrublets.

lax spread out and drooping; usually growing close to the ground.

lobe a part or segment of an organ (e.g. leaf, petal) that is deeply divided from the rest of the organ but not separated.

locule a chamber or cavity in the ovary containing one or more seeds.

midrib the central or largest vein or rib of a leaf or other organ.

naturalised an alien plant, introduced from a foreign land to a new area, where it has become established and is reproducing successfully.

nectary any structure that produces nectar, such as glands or special glandular hairs.

nutlet a small, dry, single-seeded and indehiscent fruit with a hard outer covering.

panicle a branched inflorescence with an axis that can continue to grow and does not end in a flower (i.e. the axis is indeterminate). Each branch bears two or more flowers.

papilla (plural: papillae) a soft, nipple-shaped protuberance.

pappus hairs, bristles or scales that replace the calyx in some members of the Asteraceae; they often facilitate fruit dispersal.

peltate shield-shaped; a flat structure borne on a stalk attached to the lower surface rather than to the base or margin.

perennial a plant living for three or more years.

perianth segments in this book, used for the parts of a perianth that are not, or scarcely, differentiated into calyx and corolla; segments either sepal- or petal-like (= tepals).

persistent remaining attached and not falling off.

pod a general term applied to any dry and many-seeded dehiscent fruit, formed from one unit or carpel.

pollination the transfer of pollen from the anther to the stigma.

pollinium (plural pollinia) a mass of coherent pollen grains transported as a single unit during pollination, as in members of the Asclepiadaceae and Orchidaceae.

prostrate with stems trailing or lying flat on the ground, but not rooting (= procumbent).

raceme an inflorescence in which the flowers are borne consecutively along a single (unbranched) axis, the lowest on the axis being the oldest. Each flower has a stalk.

radiate the flower heads of the Asteraceae that possess ray florets.

reflexed bent abruptly downward or backward.

rhizome a creeping (± horizontal) underground stem that sends up new stems and leaves each season.

rosette an arrangement of leaves radiating from a crown or centre, usually at ground level.

scales any thin, flat, often membranous structure.

scalloped the margin notched with rounded or broad and blunt teeth or projections (= crenate, crenulate).

shrub a perennial woody plant with usually two or more stems arising from or near the ground; differs from a tree in that it is smaller and does not possess a trunk or bole.

shrublet a low-growing perennial with stems that are woody mainly towards the base; usually less than 1 m high, and often ± prostrate (= subshrub, undershrub).

simple leaf with only a single blade.

spadix a spike with small flowers crowded on a thickened axis.

spathe a large bract that is sometimes leaf- or petal-like and encloses the young flower or inflorescence.

spike an inflorescence with stalkless flowers arranged along an elongated, unbranched axis.

spine a hard, sharply pointed structure, often long and narrow. Usually a modified leaf or stipule.

spur a tubular or sac-like projection of a flower, as from the base of a petal or sepal; it usually contains nectar-secreting glands.

taxon a group, unit, or rank of classification, for example, a species, a genus or a family.

tendril a slender, usually coiling part of the leaf or stem that serves to support the stem; a climbing organ.

tepals see perianth segments.

terminal at the tip (= apical, or at the distal end).

tuber an underground swollen part of a stem or root, which stores food; capable of producing new shoots from buds on its surface.

tubercles a small tuber-like swelling or projection.

ultramafic rocks volcanic rocks that give rise to soils with a high magnesium:calcium ratio and high concentrations of toxic heavy metals.

umbel an umbrella-shaped inflorescence in which the flower stalks all arise from the top of the main stem.

undulate with a wavy margin.

venation the pattern of veining on a leaf blade.

weed an aggressive, problem plant that usually colonises disturbed habitats and cultivated lands.

wing any thin, flat extension of an organ, as in winged fruit or seed.

PARTS OF A FLOWER

stamen { anther, filament }

perianth { petal (part of corolla), sepal (part of calyx) }

pistil { stigma, style }

ovary
ovule
locule

pedicel

ASCLEPIADACEAE (MILKWEED FAMILY) FLOWER

corona lobes

site of pollinia pair (concealed)

POLLINIA PAIR (ENLARGED)
gland (corpusculum)
translator arm
pollinium

petals

FLOWER SYMMETRY

regular

irregular

FABACEAE (PEA FAMILY) FLOWER

standard petal
calyx
wing petal
keel petal

ASTERACEAE (DAISY FAMILY) RADIATE FLOWER HEAD

ray floret
disc floret
united anthers
stigma
corolla (united petals)
interior ovary
involucral bracts

FURTHER READING

Fabian, A. & Germishuisen, G. 1997. *Wild flowers of northern South Africa*. Fernwood Press, Vlaeberg.

Joyce, P. 1999. *MTN Flower Watch: A Guide to the Cape's Floral Wonders*. Struik New Holland Publishers, Cape Town.

Le Roux, P.M., Kotzé, C.D. & Nel, G.P. 1994. *Bossieveld: Grazing plants of the Karoo and karoo-like areas*. Department of Agriculture & National Botanical Institute, Pretoria, South Africa.

Pooley, E. 1998. *A Field Guide to Wild Flowers: KwaZulu-Natal and the Eastern Region*. Natal Flora Publications Trust, Durban.

South African Wild Flower Guides, by various authors. 1: Namaqualand; 2: Outeniqua, Tsitsikamma & eastern Little Karoo; 3: Cape Peninsula; 4: Transvaal Lowveld & Escarpment; 5: Hottentots Holland to Hermanus; 6: Karoo; 7: West Coast; 8: Southern Overberg; 9: Nieuwoudtville, Bokkeveld Plateau and Hantam; 10: Cedarberg, Clanwilliam & Biedouw Valley. Botanical Society of South Africa, Claremont.

Van Wyk, B. & Malan, S. 1997. *Field Guide to the Wild Flowers of the Highveld*. Struik Publishers, Cape Town.

INDEX TO PLANT SPECIES

141